Literacy for Empowerment

Literacy for Empowerment:
The Role of Parents in Children's Education

Concha Delgado-Gaitan

The Falmer Press
(A member of the Taylor & Francis Group)
New York • Philadelphia • London

UK   The Falmer Press, Falmer House, Barcombe, Lewes, East Sussex, BN8 5DL

USA   The Falmer Press, Taylor & Francis Inc., 1900 Frost Road, Suite 101, Bristol, PA 19007

© C. Delgado-Gaitan 1990

First published 1990

British Library Cataloguing in Publication Data
Delgado-Gaitan, Concha
  Literacy for empowerment.
  1. United States. Schools. Students. Literacy
  I. Title
  379′.24
  ISBN 1–85000–662–8
  ISBN 1–85000–663–6 pbk

Library of Congress Cataloging in Publication Data are available on request
Delgado-Gaitan, Concha.
  Literacy for empowerful/Concha Delgado-Gaitan.
  p. cm.
  Includes bibliographical references.
  ISBN 1–85000–662–8
  ISBN 1–85000–663–6 (pbk)
  1. Mexican American children — Education — California — Case studies.
  2. Literacy — California — Case studies. I. Title.
  LC2687.C2D45 1990
  371.976872′0794 — dc20
  89-38892 CIP

Jacket design by Caroline Archer

Typeset in 11/13 Bembo by
Bramley Typesetting Limited, 12 Campbell Court, Bramley, Basingstoke, Hampshire.

Printed and bound in Great Britain by Taylor & Francis (Printers) Ltd, Basingstoke, Hampshire.

Jacket design by Caroline Archer

Contents

Dedication

To my mother and father,
my first teachers

Acknowledgments

Parts of the study presented in this book were made possible through research grants from the Linguistic Minority Research Project, the Pearl Chase Fund and University of California Mexus Grant. Preparation of the manuscript was made possible with support from the UCSB Faculty Career Development Award and the University of Alaska, Fairbanks Department for Rural Development.

With respect to the contents of this book, first and foremost I am deeply grateful to Henry Trueba for his critical feedback on the manuscript. Special appreciation is also owed to Robert Keatinge, Martha Allexsaht-Snider, Alina Rodriguez and Frances Escobar for their assistance in parts of the research and to Mary Hauser for her review of the manuscript. These people, however, are not responsible for errors of fact or emphasis.

Introduction

The challenge for educators to prepare minority students for successful participation in the school system is dependent on the ability of the schools to incorporate the parents and the culture of the home as an integral part of the school instruction plan. The concept of literacy and empowerment discussed in this study challenges the stereotypes often attributed to Mexican families in the United States particularly in regard to their participation in schools. Mexicans (both students and their families) have been criticized for being passive, inactive and uncaring about education and unwilling to participate in the educational system in the United States. Language has been regarded as the one obstacle for limited-English-speaking parents and held as a major source of student academic failure and the inability of parents to assist their children at home. The Portillo study allows us to see how some families, schools and one community defy the stereotypic constraints and become empowered by their collective work toward building educational opportunities for Mexican children in the home and the school.

Sarah Lawrence Lightfoot (Harvard University) in a Public Broadcasting Station interview with Bill Moyers encouraged researchers to depict the positive things that were happening in education and not just dwell on the negative. The Portillo study in no way attempts only to portray the 'positive' about the families and schools involved. Life is not a fantasy tale especially for poor and disenfranchised limited-English-speaking people and the people and the community members who struggle to help them to participate more actively in this society. It does emphasize, however, the way in which families and the schools in Portillo present a ray of hope for the possible as a result of the conscious collective involvement of families and educators.

In the study I initially resisted utilizing the concept of empowerment to analyze the findings because of the different connotations that such a concept provokes. It has been used to mean the act of showing people how to work within a system from the perspective of the people in power. This was not the connotation, however, that most served to depict the Portillo study. Most appropriately applied to this study was the meaning of empowerment as construed by Freire (1970, 1973, 1985) and Freire and Macedo (1987) in work with teaching oppressed communities in Third World countries to become socially and politically conscious about their role and status in their society through literacy. The issues of empowerment raised by Barr *et al.* (1984), Bronfenbrenner (1979) and Cochran and Woolever (1983), who showed the potential of cultural home tasks in socializing parents to become more effective agents in their children's lives while realizing the value of collective organization to balance the power relations, are important to this investigation. LeVine and White (1986) utilize the concept of empowerment without referring to it as such in their concern for culturally relative sponsorship of an individual's education by parents, teachers and other mentors who commit themselves to the realization of the individual's potential. Their emphasis on the collaborative process shows the possibility of policy implementation for an entire population so as to achieve change in the system that governs them. A crucial contribution of the empowerment theory is that it enables us to recognize that language, culture and class position need not constrain individuals or a group from actively participating in their social environment when controlling institutions (family and school) cooperate with each other to maximize the individual's influence over his/her own life. The levels of interaction that promote empowerment can be accomplished at a community meeting, a parent meeting or in a folkstory related to children by a parent or the classroom lesson, as Freire and Macedo (1987) and Moll and Diaz (1987) illustrate in their discussion of literacy.

I would not be so arrogant as to presume that the concept of literacy and empowerment is new, but a new significance can be found in the failure of the educational system in which Mexican children participate. Using this premise, the academic failure of many Mexican children is conceived of as a systemic and not a personal problem. The study in Portillo provides a window through which we can examine the process of literacy and empowerment for theoretical as well as applied purposes.

I learned a great deal from conducting this study during three years spent in the homes, the school and the Portillo community at large. Before I began the study, I viewed the concepts of literacy and empowerment as merely theoretical notions illustrated by other researchers and theorists in their respective communities. The notion of culturally determined means of academic success for linguistic minority children and their families seemed only possible through an agenda dictated by the controlling agents. The Portillo study helped me to better understand how theory derives from practice and vice versa in real field settings. The relationship between the two is fundamentally important in describing the process of literacy and empowerment because the social setting cannot be isolated from theory when one is studying issues of social relevance. To depict participants in their natural setting means utilizing the people's own words; because the group in this study is primarily Spanish-speaking, their words are represented in Spanish first and then English. Although real names would add to the portrayal of the community's real life, in order to protect individual participants' privacy I chose to use pseudonyms for participants and any other proper nouns that identified the community and any of its property.

Throughout the research I saw how the importance of what I was studying could only be described on a moment to moment basis. The people changed and their conditions changed so rapidly in many cases that it would be an injustice to use the present tense for fear that the audience would interpret it in a static way. Therefore, to depict the essence of the cultural process and change I used the past tense. I saw this as the best way to avoid constraining the description.

Because adults and children in the twenty families in this study self-identify themselves as 'Mexican', they will be referred to as such. The data examples in the text are presented in the language which the people used during the observations and interviews because the use of the native language helps to maintain the cultural integrity of the activities. The informants' original text was translated into English for the audience. Some research studies refer to the Mexican group as 'Mexican American' without reference to language proficiency; in those cases I will use the respective researcher's language to refer to the ethnic group rather than imposing my own label. Mexican is included in the broader label of 'Latino' which embraces other Spanish-speaking groups. For more extensive discussion of this issue see Garcia and Maldonado (1982) who deal with the different types of Mexican origin groups. Portes and Truelove (1987) also examine diversity among United States Spanish-speaking groups and describe the sociological status of the various groups. In this book the word 'Latino' is used to describe the parent group as defined by the Spanish-speaking parents involved in it. The parents used the term 'Latino' to identify themselves in a broader context than Mexican, and to make the organization's name into an acronym, COPLA, which stands for a title in Spanish, 'Comite de Padres Latinos'. The word 'copla' in Spanish means couplet of variable length in a popular song. The term 'Mexican' is also consistent with the group's ethnic self-identification defined by their Spanish-speaking ability and their immigrant status. Other Spanish-speaking members of the community may or may not be Mexican and their identification is noted accordingly, as in the case of Mexican children or members of the community who no longer speak Spanish.

The book is directed not only to researchers but also to school personnel who deal with Spanish-speaking families at different academic levels. The findings represent a part of these people's lives which they kindly shared with me; the book also represents their lives only at a particular time. It does not attempt to make a statement about these families, the schools or the community as a static entity. Therefore, readers should be mindful of the period in these people's lives in which the events occurred. Linguistic, cultural and social changes occur through people's interaction with one another, and those interactions characterize much of the activity in Portillo. The research presented here should not be used to stereotype participants. Rather, the purpose is to understand how one group responds to a new culture and how the seeds of effort and commitment take hold in families as it is realized that children reap the benefits of parents' help. The study depicts the meaning of life of these people, their enormous hope and the potential reality of accomplishment that results from their commitment to organize for the purpose of mutual support. This study really has no conclusion except that which has been determined as an appropriate closure for the questions raised. The lives of these people extend beyond the confines of this study and will continue while we use the information in it to understand how the process of literacy and empowerment develops, the conditions that foster it, the sociocultural changes that occur as people learn how to integrate literacy into their life experience. There is a relative as well as a universal aspect to this story. It is not just a study about a group of Spanish-speaking families. It depicts the caring and the hopes of a group of people in a difficult situation extending beyond perceived limitations to help achieve the institutional change necessary for their children to have the opportunities they should be afforded.

The book focuses on twenty families in the Portillo community and their concern with their children's academic success in literacy. The families represent a sector of the Mexican Spanish-speaking community whose children were in different reading groups in the second and third grade. The research documented activities in the context of classroom literacy lessons, home literacy-related experiences, including homework and parental interactions with the school. The major research question was how the Spanish-speaking parents assisted their children in the education process, and how those parents socialized each other to maximize their potential in dealing with the school.

Chapter 1 describes the community, Portillo, in its past and present efforts to deal with changing demographic factors in the School District. The twenty families are introduced, as are the School District's programs that serve the community as a whole and in particular the Spanish-speaking group.

Chapter 2 describes the research setting, explains how the research design was formulated and the rationale for using ethnographic methodology. Specific issues of research and advocacy are also presented.

Chapter 3 discusses the theoretical framework of literacy and empowerment. Research literature on literacy and parent involvement is presented to show how various models of parental involvement benefit the families and the school through differential levels of participation for specific purposes. More importantly, the meaning of the different strata of participation is examined in relation to the level of empowerment.

Chapter 4 defines the literacy activities of the twenty children in their respective classrooms. It introduces the second and third grade activities that socialize Spanish-speaking children to literacy at Marina elementary school. The outcomes of differential instruction practices in the classroom are shown in reference to the two different reading groups.

Chapter 5 introduces home literacy-related activities. Language and cognitive development and knowledge transmission characterize the activities that spanned topics from folkstories to family discussions about the value of schooling.

Chapter 6 investigates homework as an important arena of parental involvement as these families attempt to comply with the school's expectations to help the children in daily homework tasks. Children in both the reading groups studied do homework. The role of homework as a vehicle of parents' ability to communicate with teachers about the work and their children's academic status revealed a great deal about the critical nature of parental involvement outside the home.

Chapter 7 details the school's efforts to involve parents in an attempt to ensure some school-family contact. Parents assess their role in traditional school activities and their need for more day-to-day understanding of how the school operates.

Chapter 8 documents the process Spanish-speaking parents use to assume a leadership role in their effort to learn more about the schools and how to work with their children. Their goal was not just to help themselves but to reach out to others who may have even less experience in communicating with the schools. This process of organizing themselves into a District committee for Spanish-speaking parents can only be described as empowerment.

Chapter 9 presents theoretical, practical and policy implications in the area of home–school relationships involving literacy and parental involvement.

Chapter 1

Portillo: A Community Responding to Diversity

The setting was a regularly scheduled Portillo School District Board meeting on the first Tuesday of the month. Ten people from the community sat in a small board room in the Portillo School District office. Except for one District teacher and myself the rest of the audience were Anglo. They were present to hear the school board discuss issues dealing with school programs, including the approval of two proposals for federal funds. The two women and five men on the board were all Anglo. The board heard an elaborate presentation of achievement results by the preschool administration. The Spanish preschool was deemed successful. Little discussion ensued. The facts spoke for themselves and the board unanimously approved submitting the proposal for continued funding of this project.

Next on the agenda was the approval of a proposal for federal funding of a project for Spanish-speaking families. I presented the findings of this study that I had conducted on home and school literacy practices of Spanish-speaking Mexican children and its integral relationship to parental involvement in the schools. The proposal called for a family community learning center to be established in which the Spanish-speaking families would take literacy classes in Spanish and in English. They would also work with other parents at the center and learn ways of working with their children and the schools. The board listened attentively and one member asked a question dealing with separation of funds between the university and the District. At that point an Anglo man in the audience stood up, identified himself as a parent of two children in the district and commented,

> I think what you're proposing is commendable because it's very important for parents who feel isolated to have programs that help them feel like they belong in the schools and in the

community. If the Mexican parents do not know how to work with the schools, then it's terrific that you're trying to help them. I think that when these parents feel good about helping their children, they'll help participate in the schools, and when they do that they'll participate in the community business and that way they're participating in the development of the community.

These general sentiments about building awareness and participation among a socially and linguistically isolated sector in Portillo describe much of the social, economic and educational environment in which we studied home and school literacy interactions between adults and children. How the Spanish-speaking Mexican families live, work, learn how to assist their children in school and to empower themselves are the primary foci of the research presented here.

Living in Portillo

A few miles south of Santa Barbara, California, nestled between the Pacific Ocean and the Santa Paula mountain range lies Portillo, a small city of about 12,000 people. As one heads south on Highway 101, four exits lead to Portillo, and the freeway divides the town into an east and a west side. The streets bordering the freeway are a collage of businesses, older run-down small apartments, middle-class tract homes and a new condominium complex. Closer to the beach area homes look more like summer homes in a beach resort; this is because Portillo grew into a small city from a small beach town get-away for wealthy people from southern California cities, which are less than two hours away.

Small Town America

The Chumash (also referred to as Canalino) Indians first called it Mishopshnow. When Cabrillo landed in 1547, he found the Chumash Indians industriously building 'tomols' (plank canoes) in a valley they called 'La Portillo' (Caldwell, 1979). Rogers and other anthropologists found that three distinct Indian cultures occupied the Portillo Valley: the Oak Grove, the Hunting People and the Chumash (Stockton, 1960). These three groups of Indians had at least twelve villages in Portillo Valley, some of them built on the ruins of those gone before. They were primarily hunters. As time and White influence intervened, epidemics reduced the Hunting People population, and those remaining merged with the

Chumash. The Chumash are thought to have been excellent fishers, and they built canoes similar to those of the Polynesians and the Aleuts in Alaska (Stockton, 1960:9). A few Chumash Indians still live in the surrounding Valley area and continue to fight land policies that attempt to build on holy burial grounds.

The completion of the Southern Pacific Railroad in 1887 replaced the passenger stagecoaches that made trips from Los Angeles into Santa Barbara and stopped in Portillo. The arrival of the railroad brought with it lemon production. Until then lemons had only been grown as a small part of every family orchard. Shortly afterward, in 1889, avocados were introduced. With the need for labor in these orchards and fields and the establishment of the railroad, there was an influx of foreign labor into Portillo, leading to its first expansion. Avocados are now in such abundance that Portillo recently became the home of an annual avocado festival.

In 1925 a second major population shift occurred in Portillo as new attractive homes were built which brought wealthy residents into the area. World War II was responsible for still more development in the Portillo Valley. Red Cross offices and sewing rooms were established to assist in the war effort for soldiers quartered at the beach.

Portillo's past resembles that of other small towns in America according to some of its long-time residents. In the mid-1940s Portillo had only about 1000 residents, which helped to give it a friendly small town character. People enjoyed being recognized by the owners and other townspeople when they walked into the small shops which have long existed in Portillo. To this day townspeople disagree about maintaining the blacksmith shop which would help to retain the small town character. Until recently most of the residents lived and worked in Portillo; only a few resided outside the area and had summer homes in Portillo.

While many Mexican people lived in Portillo in the 1940s the Bracero Program in the 1950s opened the doors for even more Mexicans who came to Portillo to work. They picked lemons and avocados and worked in the nurseries and packing houses in town. In the 1960s ranches owned mainly by Japanese, Dutch and a few Mexican people also provided employment for many Mexicans as well as others. Although Mexicans had lived here for many generations, many more continued to immigrate to Portillo.

With the exception of the newly arrived Mexicans, those living in the area for generations spoke English in school and Spanish at home. The term 'Mexican', however, was considered a derogatory word to identify the Spanish-speaking community. Instead, Mexican people were usually referred to as Spanish people. By the end of the 1940s, the schools had integrated Mexican students with White students—a new phenomenon. Mexican informants who have lived in Portillo since 1920 and been community activists commented on the fact that language and ethnic barriers in Portillo have diminished over the years as a result of community services to the Mexican community that recognized the importance of language and culture.

In the 1950s a hardworking, resourceful family named Marvin moved into Portillo. Mr and Mrs Marvin, or Ma and Pa Marvin as they were called, played a significant role in the integration of many Mexican boys into mainstream culture. It is not known why only boys were selected by the Marvins to participate in the outings, but the boys became an organized group headed by Ma and Pa, called the Circle-B Boys. The boys' ages ranged from 5 to 15 years and 90 per cent were Mexican and 10 per cent were White. The Marvins were very involved in the Catholic Church and they had a monthly breakfast at the church to which they invited boys from low socioeconomic familes. Following communion, Ma and Pa arranged for rolls, hot chocolate, singing and fun. The Marvins planned outings for bus loads of Mexican boys to the zoo, carnivals and other places. People heard about the work that the Marvins did and offered to send a boy to summer camp. Financial and other resources flowed in from private families, including some Mexican contributors. No boy ever had to stay home from a field trip for lack of funds.

Smaller groups of boys were invited by the Marvins to visit homes of wealthy families in Portillo who welcomed them, invited them to use the game rooms and pool and always provided a lunch. Boys were rotated so that all of them had an opportunity to visit these homes. The unforgettable moments recounted by the boys show that they meant more than just a Sunday outing. The contact with the Marvins and their friends represented a sense of hope that they could aspire to achieve beyond their limited socioeconomic conditions. Several of the boys who participated actively in the Circle-B Boys' Club went on to do well in school and to become professionals in the community. One is a physician, two are attorneys, one is a journalist and two are teachers, one of whom earned a PhD. Other boys who did not become professionals were able to become productive citizens in the community.

The social and economic movement of many other Mexican families besides those involved with the Marvins has been evident over the years as families who lived in little shacks in the old part of town in the 1940s moved across the freeway to the newer section. However, sometimes more than one family has joined finances and shares a house. While many Mexican families have improved their socioeconomic conditions, informants believed that issues like childcare, housing for low-income people, education that will discourage students from dropping out and medical services for low-income families remain as challenges for the entire community to solve.

Present Day Portillo

The center of town consists of two perpendicular streets where several small restaurants, drug stores, clothing shops, antique shops and other retail stores provide residents with necessary daily provisions. Three of Portillo's six schools, Marina and Jackson elementary schools and the junior high school, are in this area on the west side of the freeway.

The east side of the freeway has newer single family dwelling developments and fewer small businesses. Small private ranches exist in this part of town. The three other schools are on the east side of the freeway, two elementary schools and the high school.

Of the nearly 12,000 residents, Whites represent 67 per cent, Mexicans 31 per cent, Asians 1 per cent, Blacks 0.5 per cent and others including American Indians 0.5 per cent (US Census, 1981). The Mexican population includes English-only speakers, bilingual speakers and limited-English speakers. The majority of this group (70 per cent) is English-speaking and has lived in the community for three or more generations. Although the census refers to this population as 'Spanish', the participants identified themselves as 'Mexican'.

The majority of the immigrant Mexican community lives in the west part of town where there are many more low-income rentals. Soaring rents in the area have created a devastating financial burden for most renters in the Portillo community, but even more so for working-class Mexican families since their incomes are less than those of the Anglos. For example, the family mean yearly income was between $1000 and $6000 higher for an Anglo family than a Mexican family (see Table 1).

In a two-parent family both spouses are often employed full-time in an unpredictable labor market. The average family income for a Mexican family with three children who had Spanish as their dominant language was less than $13,000 in 1987 according to the personal survey conducted with Mexican families. In essence, where these families live depends largely on their income, which in turn depends on their employment, which is highly influenced by their school attainment. The census data about Portillo revealed that the Mexican population was overrepresented in farming and fishing compared to their Anglo counterparts. For example, the total employed Anglo group over 16 years

Table 1 Family Income Characteristics of Portillo's White and Hispanic*
Communities, 1980

	Total	White	Spanish
Mean family income by family type	**(US dollars)**		
All families	22,426	22,856	21,425
Families with children under 18	22,770	22,613	20,776
Married couple families	24,224	24,730	22,176
Married couples with own children under 18	26,007	27,233	22,185
Single female households	12,692	13,122	14,154
Single female households with own children under 18	10,016	10,372	4,188
Number of families	2,863	2,356	723
Household income by monthly owners costs as percentage of income — median			
	(Percentages)		
Earning less than $10,000	32	34	50
Earning $10,000–$19,999	18	17	28
Earning $20,000 or more	16	17	12

Note:* Census data use the term 'Spanish' to identify people of Hispanic origin.
Because the term 'Spanish' can be confused with the language, the
bureaucratic term has been used here to identify the population.

of age was 4257 compared with 1668 Mexican persons. Of the employed,
almost 30 per cent of the Anglo group were managers or professionals,
while less than 9 per cent of the Mexican group occupied comparable
positions (see Table 2). US Census data show that high school graduation
of White persons over 25 was 35 per cent of the total White population
of 5343, while in the Mexican group 27 per cent graduated from a total
of 1539 in that group. Regarding college completion, the Anglo group
had 17 per cent of 5343 total in that age group compared with 5 per
cent of the total 1530 Mexicans who completed high school.

Community Service Organizations

Community organizations exist in Portillo to provide social services to
all families in the community who request them. Both the Anglo and
Mexican groups make use of these services, but some more than others
depending on the type of service that the agency offers. Both groups
use the public schools more than any other social institution in the
community.

The majority of the books in the public library are in English and
thus provide more of a service to the Anglo group than to the Mexican
group. Although few Spanish books for children and even fewer for adults

are available in the public library, some Mexican parents often took their children to the library during the summer to check out books.

The Advocacy Center provides a convenient service, particularly for Mexican adults, to have legal and personal papers translated when there are no bilingual members in a family. Family health services include counseling for alcoholics and child abusers. Anglos frequent this agency more than do Mexicans. These community services have attempted to reach the Spanish-speaking group, but the offices report less use by Mexicans. Some of this outreach occurred through the Portillo School District Migrant Program. The coordinator requested that representatives of this agency make a presentation to the parents at one of their monthly night meetings.

Legal services for the Mexican group do not exist in Portillo. During the amnesty period those people seeking assistance had to go to an agency in Santa Barbara or Oxnard. The Migrant Program in the Portillo School District, however, brought in experts on the new legal requirements to speak to the parents.

Working in Portillo

Agriculture, fishing, an aluminium factory, small private businesses and the Public School District are the primary sources of employment for Portillo residents, although some people work out of town in Santa Barbara or Ventura. Employment is variable for working-class Mexican people due to the non-permanent nature of the work, but agriculture provides the most available employment for many, primarily in small independent ranches and in local nurseries that produce orchids.

Table 2 shows that approximately 90 per cent of the bilingual and Spanish-only sector are employed in service jobs or as laborers. They are largely the immigrant Mexican group. Some Mexican people (7 per

Table 2   Profile of Employment of Portillo's White and Hispanic* Population

Occupation	Total	Percentage of Hispanic to total	Percentage of White to total
Total population	5483		
Managerial/professional	1724	7	26
Service occupation	822	7	11
Farming, fishing	318	4	2
Operators, fabricators	908	79	68
Unemployed percentage of total population	6	2	5

*Note: See note to Table 1.

cent) have become professionals and are employed in education in the Portillo School District or in small businesses.

Schooling Children in Portillo

Portillo School District serves just over 2000 students (see Table 3 for the ethnic composition of total enrolments). Approximately 35 per cent are Hispanic, of whom limited–English–speaking students comprise 40 per cent.

Portillo hired a new superintendent in 1986. He has made an impact on the district instructional program largely due to his decentralized administration. Principals are responsible for their school programs and are supported in developing new programs. The superintendent works with a small staff including a Special Projects Director, Budget Director and a small number of other coordinators who have offices in one of the schools. The ethnic composition of the school district central administration is Anglo with the exception of one Mexican male who coordinates the Migrant Program.

Portillo has six schools: four elementary, one junior high and a high school. One of the elementary schools is actually in Creekside, a community adjacent to Portillo. It serves the local Creekside community and is administered by the Portillo School District. The elementary schools are divided by grades as follows: Maple School has preschool to second grades; Marina has third to sixth grades; Jackson has third to sixth grades; and Creekside has third to sixth grades but serves mostly students in the Creekside community. The three elementary schools are administered by Anglo women principals and the secondary schools by Anglo men.

All the schools in Portillo receive state and federal funds, requiring the development of a yearly school plan. This school-site plan guides the programs which the school executes during the year. Principals must develop programs in accordance with the regulations of the special funds that supplement the school district's fiscal allocations for instruction and

Table 3   Public School Enrolment in Portillo: Ethnic Composition (percentages of total enrollment in the School District)

	1975–76	1983–84	1988–89
Hispanic	31.61	34.75	35.76
Black	0.34	1.24	1.57
Other Minority	1.87	2.40	2.22
White	66.18	62.14	60.45

Source: Data made available by the Portillo School District administration.

other programs. The process of obtaining input to develop the school plan varies among schools. Essentially, the school principals obtain input from parents, teachers and specialists to write the various components of the plan. They call meetings or survey the different sectors to assess the needs and opinions on reading, language arts, the mathematics curriculum, as well as teacher education, bilingual education and parent education.

Each school deals with the specific requirements of the following state and federal program funds: Chapter I, Economic Impact Aid (EIA), State Preschool, School Improvement Program, Special Education, Migrant Education. The planning and coordination of the specific requirements for expenditure of these funds with the programmatic needs that treat the students' identified educational programs constitute a large part of the principal's responsibility. They solicit assistance through input from teachers and parents to the extent that they help to determine the curriculum used in the classroom and events that require expenditure of state and federal funds.

Programs for Spanish-Speakers

Preschool

The Portillo School District Preschool has enjoyed state and national recognition for its progressive, creative and effective educational program offered to English and Spanish speakers. Prior to 1982, when the operation of the preschool program became a part of the Portillo School District, children attended either the Head Start program or the Community Day Care Center. Subsequently, only the Community Day Care Center co-existed with the District Preschool Program. A preschool program existed for English-only students as well as a separate bilingual (English and Spanish combined) program for limited-English-speaking (LEP) students.

In 1982 district personnel submitted a proposal to the California State Department of Education for the development of an intensive Spanish-only preschool program (Campos and Keatinge, 1984). The achievement problem reported in the proposal identified incoming kindergarten Spanish-speaking students an average of eight points lower than their English-speaking counterparts on the School Readiness Inventory, a district-wide screening measure. The scores were registered despite the fact that the test was administered to all students in their dominant language. Spanish-speaking children often mixed English and Spanish in the Head Start or Community Day Care Center which they attended prior to kindergarten. According to the authors of the Spanish Immersion Preschool Proposal, mixing the two languages may influence the students' linguistic and cognitive development, rendering them less prepared for kindergarten. Their proposed solution to this problem was the establishment of a Spanish-only preschool that could bring Spanish-speaking students to a readiness level comparable to their English-speaking peers (Campos and Keatinge, 1984).

In 1984 the program evaluation registered test scores that indicated a major success. Language, pre-literacy and cognitive skills scores on the readiness inventory showed such an increase that the gap between English- and Spanish-speaking preschool children had virtually disappeared. Students who remained in a bilingual preschool, where English and Spanish were mixed, showed no gain in the district inventory.

Two major components in the monolingual Spanish preschool contributed to its success. The first was the integration of language into a variety of culturally congruent instructional activities focused on teacher-child interaction. There was a high level of interaction between the teacher and students. Students used language to share ideas, learn new concepts and think creatively, solving problems that used their daily cultural experience. The learning principle reflected the relationship between language and cognition. The students were taught primarily in Spanish, which enhanced their first language skills and their concept knowledge in that language. Strong linguistic and cognitive development in the primary language enables students better to comprehend English when exposed to it (Cummins, 1986; Hakuta and Diaz, 1985).

The second major characteristic of this preschool involved the education of parents to be co-teachers for their children. While this may seem a commonsense course to take in a successful preschool program, it was particularly difficult and necessary in this situation where the majority of parents had less than a sixth grade education in Mexico and little or no experience in United States schools. Mrs Baca, the preschool teacher, assumed the role of parent educator so that parents were taught how to reinforce the school curriculum at home through creative activities with their children.

Parents were brought to the school on a monthly basis and taught how to implement a child-centered curriculum in their home through their daily activities. For example, at Christmas Mrs Baca held several meetings with parents to teach them, among other things, how to shop for educational toys by comparing them with the cost of typical commercial toys. Parents were convinced of the monetary savings for the family. Through training such as this, parents became knowledgable and confident in helping their children at home. The teacher kept them appraised of their children's learning on almost a daily basis. Therefore, parents learned what was expected of them, they stayed informed about their children's learning and they became involved by attending school meetings and helping their children learn at home.

Bilingual Program

Learning in English and Spanish became an issue for Portillo prior to the development of the Spanish-only preschool. Bilingual education in Portillo initially meant primary language instruction for English and Spanish dominant students in the same classroom, and a bilingual teacher used both languages to instruct according to the student's language needs. The bilingual program served preschool through sixth grade. Student materials for reading were purchased for Spanish-speaking students and the School District made an effort to hire bilingual teachers. Unfortunately, Spanish material was often not of the same high quality as that in the English program. For example, in one second grade the English-speaking students read the complete novel, *Little House on the Prairie*, while Spanish-speakers read short stories in a Spanish-reading textbook without the experience of reading a novel. The teachers complained that part of the problem was that novel-like books did not exist in Spanish. This was a built-in inequity in the system for Spanish-speakers.

Another problem in the Portillo bilingual program (as in many other California districts) was that some bilingual teachers left before the district was able to replace them with other equally experienced bilingual personnel. Due to materials and personnel problems, the program lost its effectiveness in the upper grades (fourth through sixth) until well trained bilingual teachers could be found. At a meeting of Mexican parents a couple of parents complained to the Special Projects Director about the need for bilingual teachers who were fully literate in Spanish; they were upset that their children were being taught incorrect Spanish language use.

In spite of all of the problems that many bilingual programs face with respect to funding, personnel training and curriculum, in recent years this School District has had the advantage of a few effective and supportive administrators, including a new superintendent, Director of Special Projects, and two principals, all of whom are bilingual.

In 1987 the Director of Special Projects and the principal at Maple School expanded the Spanish preschool model to first and second grades. One kindergarten was already in place which had achieved excellent results in the district tests. In the Spanish-only classes the students were paired with students from English-only classes for English as a Second Language lessons. Thus two distinct bilingual program models were implemented in Portillo through the second grade. Another Spanish-only class was being planned for Jackson School to begin in the fall of 1988.

Two models co-existed, the mixed English and Spanish classes and the Spanish-only model. The district had not assessed the effectiveness of the new model through tests, but the Director of Special Projects obtained qualitative data. The interaction analysis indicated that Mexican children in the Spanish-only classes interacted more frequently with each other on academic related topics and interacted more like equals with English-only counterparts in tasks where two students of each language group were paired together to problem-solve.

There were variations in teachers' use of English and Spanish in the classroom, in levels of teacher–student interaction, in peer interaction, direct instruction and creativity. A clear distinction, however, was made between teachers who utilized literature-based reading and writing instruction. This method supposedly encouraged students to read and discuss literary works more than the traditional textbook method which restricted students to reading the commercial textbook. Teachers complained that the Spanish textbooks were usually boring and unimaginative. The principals and the teachers decided on the type of reading program for their school. Although the literature-based literacy program has been observed to produce higher levels of teacher–student interaction, experience-based peer interaction about the stories and writing about the readings, there do not appear to be any data to suggest that basic textbook reading could not be organized to develop equally high levels of thinking skills, teacher–student interaction, reading and writing. The District Director of Special Programs proposed that the teachers coordinate the goals for the entire program from preschool through sixth grade to ensure that teachers provide ample opportunity to maximize the development of literacy and cognitive skills despite differences in curriculum materials used in the different schools. Both bilingual program models provide the Spanish-speaking students with opportunities to learn language and literacy and cognitive development.

Migrant Education Program

The California State Department of Education funds special programs for Spanish-speaking students whose parents work in migratory-related employment. In Portillo approximately 105 families received help from this program, which was coordinated by Mr Reyes. In addition to administering the program, he taught some of the pull-out classes in the high school for migrant students.

To receive services from this program, the adults must be employed in agriculture or fishing. Three major services were provided for qualifying families: health insurance, parent education, and academic support through tutoring. Even if parents do not participate actively in the program parent meetings or if the students do not receive supplementary tutoring, the families still take advantage of the health insurance.

Many students whose families qualify for migrant program services needed academic support. The program provided tutoring once or twice weekly through a migrant teacher assistant at each school. Theoretically, teacher assistants conferred with the classroom teachers to develop an individual learning plan for the students. Students were often tutored outside the classroom, although tutoring occasionally took place in the classroom.

The parent education part of the program brought parents together approximately every six weeks to two months to inform them about current topics of interest in the program and conferences which they might attend. According to the guidelines prescribed by the State Department of Education, the program coordinator only had to meet with parents three times during the year. However, he felt committed to make parents aware of topics pertinent to their children's education, such as alcohol in the family, AIDS, high school dropouts, scholarship information for college and immigration rights. These were presented by community agency representatives. Although this type of parent education did not involve much discussion or train parents to develop any particular skills in organizing, the parents became aware of some issues related to their welfare and to children's education.

The parents related well to the coordinator; they reported that he was the only person who guided them in solving problems with their children. While this may appear admirable on the part of the coordinator, it also makes apparent a gap in training for parents who do not know how to deal with their child's teacher or the school. Although some such knowledge was covered in the parent meetings, parents did not have a vehicle for learning these skills or for being supported in an ongoing and consistent way. It was clear that the parent coordinator could deal with questions about students in the high school where he taught. He could not, however, help them with day-to-day problems. Thus the students' problems persisted when parents could not deal with the school on their behalf.

Project Vision

Project Vision was a special program for Spanish-speaking gifted students. It was conceived by a kindergarten teacher and the Director of Special Projects. They observed the underrepresentation of limited-English-speaking Mexican children in the Gifted and Talented Education (GATE) program. Of 165 students, only 12 per cent were Mexican (Campos and Keatinge, 1987). The problem in Portillo was that the state department compliance recommendations expected 36 per cent Mexican enrolment in the program. The purpose of Project Vision was to bridge the enrolment gap that existed between Anglo and Mexican students in the District's GATE program. The goals of Project Vision were:

1 to uncover positive solutions to the problem of the identification of LEP students;
2 to gain knowledge in the instruction of potentially gifted LEP students;
3 to train the parents and teaching staff of these students;
4 to integrate the findings of the project into the district's regular GATE program.

The authors of Project Vision based their design on research by Bloom (1981), Clark (1986), DeAvila (1986) and Hunt (1971) who hold the view that 'giftedness' is influenced by the environment and therefore subject to change through environmental intervention. Environmental interaction can result in a 20–40 or more point difference in measured intelligence (Bloom, 1981; Skeels and Dye, 1959; Hunt, 1979). The project was designed to create an environment for students that would provide unlimited opportunity, experiences and choices. It followed five major suggestions in the research literature:

1 early identification and opportunities to develop individual talents and skills through interacting in a variety of stimulating environments;
2 instruments and processes to identify potential candidates;
3 training teachers to recognize potentially gifted/talented LEP students, as well as to organize their teaching to develop and expand the gifted/talented LEP student's talent;
4 training parents of potentially gifted/talented students to meet the unique needs of their gifted/talented child socially, emotionally, physically and cognitively;
5 training district support staff to recognize potentially gifted/talented students, as well as to provide support to identified students, teachers and parents (Campos and Keatinge, 1987).

At the end of the one year of this project the evaluators concluded that Mexican children in the preschool, kindergarten and first grade, were closer to their more affluent White counterparts in the GATE program on conservation scale measures than the second and third graders, who performed notably lower. The Project Vision coordinators explained that possibly the lack of access to conditions such as those of the middle/higher SES community in the School District begins to take effect after students leave first grade. Given that most, if not all, students in Project Vision had limited access to ideal conditions for competing on an equal basis, the recommendations made by the project coordinators were that the school must provide these children with the maximum environment to develop their fullest potential through their entire schooling career. Furthermore, they concluded that a strong parent voice enhanced the students' opportunity for success. Thus parents of Mexican LEP students needed to learn how the school system operated and how they, as parents, could have access to resources to help their children in home and school. This recommendation points to the high expectations which the schools hold for a strong parental role in children's school success. The need for parents to be integrally involved in their children's education calls for a systematic parent education program which helps parents become aggressive consumers of education for their children (Campos and Keatinge, 1987).

Twenty Families: A Closer Look at Life in Portillo

Much of this study centered on twenty Spanish-speaking second and third graders of Marina School and their families. These families had four areas in common: their working-class socioeconomic status, their Spanish language, their immigrant status from Mexico, and the fact that all the children began school in Portillo. Although some of the children were born in Portillo, all the parents in these families immigrated from different parts of Mexico. Many had lived in isolated rural ranches on the outskirts of larger cities like Mexico D.F. The length of residence in Portillo for these families ranged from five to thirteen years. Family composition is shown in Table 4.

Most of the families lived in the neighborhood surrounding Marina School with the exception of two who lived on the west side of the freeway. One of these families lived in a trailer court. This family owned their single room trailer and paid monthly rental space. Five family members were permanent residents there and four members of the extended family lived in the trailer temporarily. The remainder of the

Table 4 Family Composition of the Twenty Families

Family name (pseudonyms)	Number of children in home	Number of parents
Alonzo	2	2
Acosta	4	2
Hernandez	4	2
Cortina	3	2
Dominguez	5	2
Rosalez	4	2
Gomez	2	2
Suarez	4	2
Solis	6	2
Mora	4	1
Ramos	3	2
Munos	5	2
Alva	4	2
Vega	4	1
Sandoval	7	2
Toledo	2	2
Vela	2	2
Barra	5	2
Zamora	5	2
Sanchez	2	2

families rented their homes or apartments. The largest home had three small bedrooms and one bathroom with a small living room and kitchen. The homes had been built within the last three years and offered low-income rental housing. They were small and clean and sparsely furnished. One couch, a center table and a television set comprised the livng room furniture. Wall hangings with landscapes adorned the walls. Potted orchids and ceramic animal figurines filled the shelves. The kitchen usually had a small dining room table and six chairs and white appliances. Occasionally, toasters, *mocajetes* used for grinding and coffee makers sat on the sink counter. The bedrooms had beds and a small desk and chair, with a small book shelf which held a few story books in English, encyclopedia sets and comic books which parents had purchased at discount department stores, flea markets and garage sales. Although most of the families lived alone as nuclear families, many had extended family that lived nearby and visited often. The relatives were parents, brothers, nephews, cousins or friends of the adults in the families. They shared groceries, childcare, information about employment and social events such as picnics.

A few of the families lived in smaller one and two bedroom apartments. These families also tended to live as single nuclear families with extended family living nearby. Only in a couple of cases did the extended family live together with the family in the study. In those cases the one bedroom apartment was home for fifteen to eighteen people. Usually this was a temporary situation and fluctuated depending on family members who happened to be in Portillo seeking employment.

Employment varied for the adults in the twenty families. Although many worked for the same employer, their jobs differed slightly. Most of the employed adults worked as gardeners or clerks at the nurseries, in assembling at the aluminium factory, housekeeping in private homes and local motels, waiting on tables and counters at fast food businesses, custodians, and loading clerks at local print companies. Although the postions varied in nature, per household income was comparable. The median household income for these families was lesss than $13,000. The average family size was five—two parents and three children. Two of the families were single parent families. In most of these families both adults were employed and in the case of single parents they too worked. In only a couple of cases where there were two parents in the family the woman worked part-time or was unemployed. Unemployment tended to be temporary for most of these families. Adults found it necessary to work to keep food on the table. Most of them did not apply for welfare unless there was absolutely no other resort. As one parent commented, 'Aunque quieramos vivir en welfare, no es possible porque no nos dan casi nada. Es mejor tratar de conseguir cualqier trabajito y aveces mas que uno para poder mantener a la familia.' [Even if we tried to live on welfare, it's impossible because they give us so little. It's better to try and find whatever job we can get and usually more than one is necessary in order to raise a family.] Many of these adults had two and sometimes three jobs. They worked in the nurseries during the day, washed dishes at a local restaurant at night and gardened on the weekends. As an extra job many women worked as housekeepers in private homes.

Unemployment usually occurred as a result of employer decisions to reduce the labor force during low seasons at the nurseries. The adults' limited skills and lack of education required to obtain more professional positions prevented acquisition of other jobs. The majority of the adults in the twenty families had less than sixth grade education with fourth grade being the median level. Only two parents had completed high school in Mexico. Stories of the hardships in Mexico revealed the reasons for their lack of education. Most of them left school to work and help their family. Others just found the conditions extremely burdensome in terms of the end result as this parent indicated:

Mi familia vivia en un rancho y teniamos que caminar más de una hora para llegar a la escuela. Luego cuando llegavamos a la escuela las maestras nos pegaban con una varilla cuando no sabiamos una respuesta. Cuando llegue al quinto grado y me canse de ir a la escuela aunque mis padres querían que siguiera me salí. Mejor les ayudaba en en rancho y pocos años después me casé con mi esposo. [My family lived in a ranch and we had to walk over an hour to get to school. Then when we arrived at school the teachers hit us with a twig when we did not know the answers. When I got into the fifth grade I got tired and even though my parents wanted me to continue, I quit. I just stayed home and helped them on the ranch and a few years later I married my husband.]

Their lack of opportunity to be educated in Mexico contributed to their feelings of vulnerability in working and learning in the United States. Nevertheless, they all expressed a strong desire to have their children succeed. Their desire to help their children with their schooling led them to English classes. They tried to improve their skills by taking English-as-a-Second Language classes at Santa Barbara Community College. After completing the ESL program at the community college some of the adults proceeded to study for their General Education Diploma (GED) in Spanish so that they had at least one credential. Their intent was to continue studying in the community college for a specific career. This suggests that immigrant adults were making an effort to learn new skills and accommodate to the new system and aspired for a stronger position to assist their children in school.

Advocates in the Schools

While making efforts to provide quality living, working and learning conditions for all its residents, the Portillo community in general recognized its limitations in incorporating the Spanish-speaking sector of the community into the mainstream. The educational and community programs have actively dealt with providing equity and opportunity to participate in the education system. The parent training programs have been successful to the extent that advocates within the schools have been committed to work with that sector of the community.

Key personnel within the District preschool, Migrant, Project Vision and bilingual programs have played the role of advocates for Spanish-speaking students and their families. The advocate role assumed by educators communicated to students and parents in a variety of ways the extent to which the minority language and culture are valued within the context of the school (Cummins, 1986:26). The educational programs for Spanish-speaking students have been sponsored by individuals whose efforts have helped to build a supportive educational program for all students in Portillo and in particular the Spanish-speaking students.

The participation of Mexican students and their families in the educational system is related to their position in the job market and other social institutions. That is, although most of the Spanish-speaking Mexican families in Portillo were relegated to unskilled and service jobs, many held hope that the situation could change for their children if they succeeded in school. Thus the school became a strong focus for them. As some parents observed their children succeed in programs like the bilingual preschool, Project Vision, the bilingual program, and Migrant Education, their value of schooling was strengthened. When they met collectively as parents, they learned that there were advocates who could assist them in their efforts to help their children. This constitutes a form of social and cultural change. Parents learned to work collectively and cooperate with the school (Cochran and Woolever, 1983). This process of parental participation in children's schooling became the specific focus of the study developed in the subsequent chapters in this book. Spanish-speaking parents strongly value schooling for their children and they demonstrate this in a variety of ways. The problem, however, became more pronounced as parents attempted to comply with the school's expectations about parents helping their children with schoolwork. The study describes how children learned literacy in the classroom and at home and how parents attempted to make sense of what the school expected them to do to help their children succeed in school.

Chapter 2

Inside Families and Schools

Research in Portillo has involved a long-term commitment on the part of the researcher to examine problems which have no simple solutions. From the beginning the intention was to establish a cooperative arrangement with the School District which could foster the planning and implementation of the study of topics of mutual interest, since the impact of ethnographic reseach in education is most visible as a result of a long-term involvement between the researcher and a specific community.

Entry into Portillo Schools and Community

Although there has been a precedent established which allows ethnographers to study social groups to which they belong (Peshkin, 1982), a criticism often raised is that the personal experience which they bring to the field may interfere with the objective analysis of the research data (Peshkin, 1988; Wolcott, 1988). It is therefore necessary for the ethnographer to be conscious about any presumed biases which may influence the study.

In evaluating this anthropological axiom, I had to confront those issues in my background which have served as a functional duality in my academic work. My background as a Spanish-speaking Mexican woman has been both an asset and a liability in my academic work. My ability to speak the language and to earn the trust of the families stems from having grown up in a family that resembled those in the research. I have long believed that children could learn to succeed academically regardless of the family's socioeconomic and sociocultural background. Even though my family seemed so different from White middle-class families, my sisters and I all did very well in school. In retrospect I realize that it only appeared that my parents were not involved in our schooling.

What they did at home to shape a nurturing learning environment was meaningful. That tacit cultural understanding I brought to the field required the use of extensive triangulation in data collection to ensure that I had not been cavalier in my interpretation and analysis of the data by assuming that I knew what the data meant. Peshkin (1988) reminds us that owning up to our biases only means that by recognizing our subjectivity we can manage it. We can never be value-free. A technique that I have developed to assist me in this process has been to review as much of the data as possible with the participants so that the analysis can be made jointly with the researcher.

As a professor at the University of California, Santa Barbara, I have taught students who live and work in the Portillo School District. Most of them have demonstrated extensive knowledge about Portillo coupled with a sincere commitment to improve the quality of education for minority students (Campos and Keatinge, 1984; Campos and Keatinge, 1988). Their commitment, and the tenacity required to make programs that affect underrepresented groups in their schools a reality, interested and inspired me to observe their programs. As a result, I became involved in researching some of the questions that most concerned me from an academic point of view and concerned them from a practitioner's perspective. My relationship with these students also facilitated my entry into the families and the schools. They provided me with names of families, key school personnel, District data sets, and schedules of School District activities to attend.

Deciding the Research Agenda

The research agenda pursued here originated as a mutual agreement between the Portillo School District Special Projects Director and the researcher in January 1986. The reason for involving District administration in the process emerged from the need to determine an area of study which would most benefit the District as well as the academic community. A joint decision would also bear on the level of District cooperation in the study. At meetings with the Director of Special Projects I described the status of the research literature pertaining to my area of interest, while the Director discussed the District's areas of need. The area of classroom literacy alone held little interest for the School District because training in the classrooms focusing on teacher–student interactions had begun. There was a particular concern about the absence of Mexican parent involvement in the schools and a paucity of information about the family home culture. However, the topic of parental involvement had to be contextualized in a specific content area. Literacy was the appropriate subject because of the concern for achievement in reading on the part of both school and home. Thus the issue of literacy was investigated as it pertained to the relationship of Mexican parents with school. During the three years in the field I systematically examined how parents involved themselves in their children's education in respect to the acquisition of literacy.

The process of initiating an ethnographic study raises issues of theoretical grounding (Chilcott, 1987). Wolcott (1987) reminds us that ethnography is much more than mere description and that the most characteristic part of ethnography is that it discerns cultural patterning in the behavior observed. Wolcott (1988) later poses the question, 'What guides my research so that I am willing to lay claim for its anthropological orientation' (p. 20)? In applying this question to my study I first had to consider what I proposed to investigate. The topics of home-school literacy and parental involvement in Spanish-speaking children's schooling required some preliminary theoretical assumptions about issues such as cultural change, literacy acquisition, the family as a cultural unit, and the school as a cultural organization. The premise of empowerment emerged as the study progressed.

The guiding premises which were carried into the field emerged from my analysis of the recent research literature. The operational definition of literacy takes into account the ecocultural niche which is influenced by the family's socioeconomic level, social and political relations, religious beliefs, regional ecological location as well as the family's relation to other institutions including neighborhood, museums, media, health institutions and schools (Weisner, 1976, 1979, 1984). That is, literacy is a socioculturally constructed activity which varies because of different configurations that families take in different social and cultural settings. This suggests a rather expansive concept of literacy to include the socially constructed interaction in which oral language, cognitive skills, and text-related operations like reading and writing occur in the context of a personally motivated situation (Tharp and Gallimore, 1988; Trueba, 1989).

The ability to interpret linguistic and graphic symbols associated with text requires one type of ability. Literacy is a sociocultural process, and it follows that another literate ability has to do with the sociocultural knowledge and cognitive skills that are necessary for the child and the family to interpret text. The individual must understand the context of text which is part and parcel of the larger complex sociocultural system that alludes to values and specific meaning. This definition allows us to consider the wide range of activity within family literacy activities, including non-school related text and homework activities. The parents' knowledge about text and their ability to help their children to make the link between home and school literacy activities constitute the crucial relationship between literacy activities in the home and in the classroom. To the extent that parents can interpret classroom text that goes home and guide their children in dealing with it, they support their children emotionally, cognitively and linguistically. Parent communication with the school contributes to the empowerment of parents and children because parents act on behalf of their children. The process of acquisition of those skills also plays a role in the process of empowerment. (These issues will be discussed in more detail in Chapter 3).

Prior to engaging in fieldwork, I made certain theoretical assumptions on the basis of previous research. This set a baseline perspective for the collection of data. For example, it was established that families' activities were all legitimate because of their culturally-based nature. That is, parents raise their children to be competent within their own group, and the childrearing strategies utilized depended largely on access to material and human resources (Bronfenbrenner, 1979b; Ogbu, 1981b). Furthermore, given the issues of stereotypes surrounding Mexican families in the United States, it was imperative that this research study consider the cultural heterogeneity of Mexican families (Laosa, 1983), including those socialization activities that characterize the group in this study. These theoretical assumptions were carried into the field initially and were refined and extended as the research progressed.

Several research subquestions focused on particular aspects of the school and home literacy processes.

1 How do teachers organize classroom literacy activities for high and low achievers?
2 What are the different literacy activities in the home, and what is the parental role in those practices?
3 How do parents of children in the high and low reading groups compare in their involvement with their children's school?
4 How do Spanish-speaking parents learn to participate in the schools?

These research questions determined the data collection strategies and the selection of participants at each level of the study. Demographics provided a backdrop and macro-context for the study. Such data were gathered about the people in Portillo particularly in relation to the education system. Although most of the demographic data were collected from census information, interviews with Anglo and Latino elders who had been born and lived in Portillo all their life were also conducted.

The interviews provided valuable information about Portillo's past and present and supplemented the census figures.

The nature of the research questions dictated an ethnographic design and method for two main reasons: the process of social and cultural change in the families is basic to the questions, and topics such as these are best examined ethnographically in order to reveal actual practices. Ethnographic observation and interviews were the most utilized methods in studying parent involvement in children's schooling through literacy activities.

Studying Classroom Literacy Activities

Although many Spanish-speaking (LEP) students succeed academically in Portillo schools, others fail, and the results appeared most noticeable in reading scores as children moved into defined reading levels in the second and third grades. The School District's test scores showed a differential achievement pattern within the group. This pattern of achievement was the deciding factor concerning the study of literacy practices and parental involvement of students who were high and low achievers in the second and third grades. Student achievement was determined by each teacher and by the California Achievement Test (CAT) standardized scores. Classroom literacy was a necessary part of the study because it provided an insight into children's academic performance and the school's expectations of them. When the family observations and interviews were collected, my understanding of the discrepancy between school and home expectations in terms of parental role would be facilitated.

Initially the teachers did not feel comfortable having me in their classrooms. They felt that I was evaluating them. The principal intervened, and in a meeting with all those involved the principal suggested that I spend less time in the classroom. I explained to them the purpose of my observations in the classroom and offered reassurance that I was not an evaluator. I also told them that as soon as I had observed the general activities during the reading period, I would offer assistance in activities like helping children to do their seatwork. The teachers felt somewhat relieved and did not complain further about my presence in the classroom.

Twenty second and third grade Spanish-speaking students at Marina elementary school and their families were selected to participate in this study. The students represented advanced and novice reading achievement levels that were defined by the teachers. The decision to identify the students as novice and advanced readers was based on Cole and Griffin's

(1983) notion that students in the traditionally labeled 'low' groups are not necessarily low readers, rather they are beginning readers who have not been taught effectively. Advanced readers, on the other hand, have progressed beyond the novice readers because they have received instruction that gives them an advantage. Eleven students were novice readers, three in second grade and eight in third grade. Nine students. were advanced readers, five in the second grade and four in the third grade. Novice readers read at least one grade below their respective grade and advanced readers read at or above grade level.

Over five months observations of high and low achievers in reading and language arts lessons were conducted three times a week. Each observation lasted approximately one hour. Teacher interviews provided additional data on the relationships between School District policies and classroom procedures as well as on teacher perceptions of the parents' role in students' schooling.

Analysis and Reorganization of Research Focus

Following five months of data collection in the classroom the focus shifted to the home learning environments of the children. The classroom data revealed only that part of the children's literacy that was related to academic tasks. To complete the picture, it was necessary to examine how the children dealt with these and other literacy tasks at home, and how the parents played a role in informal and academic literacy activities.

Studying Family Literacy Activities

The children's families lived within a two-mile radius of Marina school. The families shared a working-class Mexican immigrant status, their Spanish language and their strong desire to have their children succeed in school. Although some of the children had been born in the United States, the parents were originally from Mexico. Aside from these common characteristics, family organization and activities differed in form and function on a day-to-day basis.

Data collection in the family setting presented few problems since the parents were most gracious and accommodating to me when I walked in loaded with video equipment. On occasion, however, families did seem apprehensive about my presence and what I might ask and see. So they gathered all of their children together and sat in the living room and only the parents talked on behalf of the family. I had to remind them that I needed to interview each member separately as much as possible and that I preferred that they went about their own activities while I was there so that I could better understand their daily routine. Another way that the interviews were problematic was the parents' cryptic responses of a word or two in answer to interview questions. In two cases telephone calls were made to keep in touch with the families and allow informal conversation so that trust could be established and they could feel more comfortable during the interviews. The interviews examined how parents assisted their children in the home on literacy tasks and were combined with observations. After school and evening hours as well as some weekends became the best times to observe how parents interacted with their children on non-academic and academic literacy tasks. Homework tasks were predictably observed just before or after dinner. Most interactions were audio-recorded and a selected few were videotaped to document any consistent pattern. Videotaping in the home required trust between the researcher and the family, which only time could build. A total of seventy-five home literacy activities were collected, ranging from twenty minutes to two hours in length.

Ethnographic interviews of parents and children included questions about their residence, employment and other demographic information, the meaning of literacy in the home, and a description of their participation in the schools. The core questions focused on skills required for their job, how much their children knew about their employment, what they expected their children to have as employment/career in the future, and what local social resources they utilized for what purpose. Interviews about specific home tasks attempted to clarify observations made in the home on the type of literacy material in the home, how adults and children participated with each other, expectations about learning literacy in school, and parental contact with the school on literacy related matters.

Extending the Study

The primary unit of analysis was the home literacy activity that included formal and informal literacy events and homework activities. The families' interactions were captured through observations that revealed the cultural practices of each family relative to their children, literacy and the school. Such interactions were analyzed within the parameters which encompass the who, what, where, when and why of the activity. The literacy activity (for example, the classroom reading group, non-school literacy related home tasks, homework lessons, the parents' communication with the school regarding their children's literacy achievement and parent organizational meetings) provided an opportunity to observe the students' and parents' ability to be competent in literacy in these contexts.

Five levels of activity organization were used to examine the interactions around literacy. The *who* refers to the persons present during the activity and available to assist the child. The *what* describes the operations that are accomplished and how they are done. The *where* refers to the place of production. The location is largely dictated by the availability of cultural tools. The *when* of the activity accounts for the time, either the length of time or frequency of the activity. The *why* refers to the meaning of the activity to the people involved in the interaction. The participants bring a set of cultural assumptions to the activity which helps to structure their goal-directed behavior. In each activity the cultural transmission process was operative as adults transmitted knowledge to children or to each other. The home activity setting was selected as a focus of observation because it portrays day-to-day culture.

Incidents depicting the operations, personnel, place of production, length of time and goals of the activities were reviewed in the data from field notes, audiotape transcriptions and videotapes for frequency of events which constituted the patterns of generalizations. These patterns were found across the literacy activities within each family, within the classroom literacy activities and within the parent meetings that dealt with their role in their children's education. Rare events were also noted and explained within the families and between children in the advanced and novice reading groups.

The analysis from this part of the study led to further examination of a phenomenon which appeared saliently in the home-school data on parent involvement in literacy activities. The classroom and home literacy activities data showed that most parents faced difficult problems in supporting their children because they lacked information about the school's expectations of them as parents. They also lacked the skills to provide maximum support for their children. This observation prompted me to pose specific questions about parent involvement and parent education for Spanish-speaking parents.

Studying Parent Involvement

To encompass the research question completely, the study was expanded to include parent meetings, with teacher/parent training sessions as a specific focus. Observations of parent meetings and training sessions provided a major part of the data on specifics of parent involvement. Observations included the bilingual preschool parent meetings, individual school parent meetings of advisory committees, school parent training workshops, Migrant Program business meetings, Project Vision parent training, informal parent-teacher contacts and the newly developed District committee of Mexican parents. Interviews of parents, administrators and teachers, as well as a teacher and parent survey, provided additional data on the nature of parent participation in the school. The various parent meetings were observed on a monthly basis between September 1986 and August 1987.

In addition, the K-6th grade bilingual teachers in the district responded to a survey soliciting information on the nature and level of contacts with parents in their respective classrooms. This was done to determine the difference in contact with the parents of children in the various reading levels.

Researcher Role in Ethnographic Research

My role as a researcher merits mention because it was an intentional position during the entire study. Furthermore, it makes a critical point about the relationship between research methodology, the researcher and the field. Ethnographic fieldwork dictums require that the researcher learn the local culture (Geertz, 1973; Spindler, 1982; Spradley, 1979) through strict interviews, observation or participation observation. This means that the researcher can participate in the culture in order to understand it from the insider's point of view and be able to describe it from the local's perspective.

I found that the observer and interviewer technique was most appropriate for the type of questions posed in this study. One of the most important features of my role was the involvement extended to participants in the research. It became important to have the insider's perspective in the analysis as much as possible, thus I shared my data with each sector (administration, families, teachers) of the community. The purpose in sharing the data, which I communicated to the participants, was to obtain an accuracy check. For example, I presented data that I collected in the classroom to the teachers and received their comments about the activities that had been observed. Not only were clarifications made but teachers became aware of certain parts of their interaction with students of which they were unaware. One teacher commented, 'I didn't know that Beto could answer so many questions correctly; I tend to think of him as a kid who never gets a correct answer cause he's not paying attention, but, look, in all of these lessons you have here, he's doing ok.' Although I did not intend that participants should change their behavior as a result of requesting feedback from them on my data, it became apparent that as a researcher, I could not control what they did with the insights they gained as a result of my sharing data with them. I met three times with teachers participating in the bilingual program in two-hour meetings. The teachers did not collectively have access to the data about the parents, although they responded individually to the family data collected in the home. Teachers usually responded defensively about the confusion which parents expressed regarding the school's expectations of them. They held strong positions that some parents cared and others did not, thus the differential student achievement. The third grade teacher commented, 'Some parents just don't want to take the time to help their kids. Other parents work just as many hours but when it comes down to their kids, they're here in a minute. Sure I feel sorry for some parents cause they just can't get it together, but I work hard here too and they just have to learn how to cooperate.' This position about parent involvement was a common one held by the K-6th grade bilingual teachers as revealed in the teacher survey.

The sharing of data occurred in an hour-long meeting with the respective parties at least once every other month. Administrators, most frequently the Director of Special Projects, Mr Clark, reviewed data collected in the classroom. His feedback was solicited because of his close involvement in bilingual teacher education and curriculum development. He commented on the accuracy of the literacy activities as he knew them to be, noted differences in the way he perceived certain activities when he observed in the classroom, and observed how important it was to get a systematic day-by-day account of the activities.

Part of the classroom data included teacher interviews about the level of support received from the administration. The Director of Special Projects had access to this anonymous data for comment. Much of the time he agreed with the teachers' perceptions about the type of assistance which teachers received in the classroom. A few times he clarified the role of principal and Director of Special Projects with respect to teacher training on new literacy techniques for bilingual teachers. He stated, 'I don't have the jurisdiction to request that teachers use a specific teaching approach without the principal's approval and I can't go over her head. I have talked with her about it and showed her evidence of places where the literature-based program has been most effective but she insists that "her" teachers have to use the basal program.' The Director of Special projects felt that he had learned more about the classroom from reviewing my classroom data. He also responded to the data on family literacy activities, 'It's incredible. I guess they do care and we need to include them more in the schools. The question of homework needs to be clarified between teachers and parents too. I have long felt that it posed many problems for everyone and causes many bad feelings for all parents.' During one meeting to review data on the family Mr Clark suggested he would like to know more about the role of the parents in the schools because that was an area to which the District had not given very much attention in recent years. We discussed at length the type of District organized activities I would need access to in order to examine in detail the issues of parental involvement. I also insisted on the opportunity to share with parents data on classroom and family literacy activities and their implications for parent education. Mr Clark consented to cooperate wherever needed to facilitate my entry to District activities.

Parent meetings of migrant education families provided the context to present my data to parents. The Director of the Migrant Program, Mr Reyes, coordinated his meetings with me and provided time for me to address the parents on different aspects of the data, such as the issue of parent knowledge about school resources to help children who have been labeled underachievers. Each meeting focused on a different part of the data — parent-teacher contact, use of community resources for family literacy development, parent skills to help children with home-work, and communicating with children about career plans.

Attendance averaged thirty adults, except for the last session when only seven people attended because the meeting was held on the day before Good Friday, a major Catholic holiday. To enhance the presentation I used overhead transparencies that graphically depicted the data. Confidentiality of the families in the study was not threatened because the data only depicted trends. Individual families were not mentioned by name, nor were personal situations detailed. Parents raised questions about their own situation and wanted direction about how to deal with their difficulties, which usually related to helping their children at home and communicating with the school. I did not provide answers directly; rather I shared information about the way that parents in the study perceived similar problems and their approach to solving them. Consistently I reminded them that I could not give them simplistic answers to their problems and that many other parents shared their concerns and felt very isolated. The tacit message was that some parents had knowledge about the school system that could be shared with others. Five meetings were held with parents and, except for the last meeting when the video camera did not function, four of the meetings were video-taped.

The last meeting produced some rather unpredictable results. One of the parents who had not been a part of the study but had been to all of my presentations stood up and remarked to Mr Reyes,

Yo creo que lo que necesitamos es un grupo de padres que actuen como lideres que pueda ayudar a otros padres que necesitan más información porque se sienten aislados. Hay aquí varias personas que sepan más que otros y pueden compartir su conocimiento para ayudarnos unos con otros. Solo necesitamos a alguien que trabaje con nosotros y nos ayude a organisarnos para ese proposito. [I think that what we need is a group of parents who need more information because they feel isolated. We have several people here who know more than others and can share their knowledge to help us all. We need someone to help us organize ourselves.]

The Director agreed with him and encouraged him to pursue his idea for organizing other parents to act as a leadership group: Having heard this parent's enthusiasm for taking responsibility to organize a parent leadership group for Spanish-speaking parents, I raised questions to the parents and to Mr Reyes about how he might approach the organization of a leadership group. Mr Reyes commented that the parents could meet and decide how to organize themselves and the topic changed to scheduling a meeting for the next Migrant Program business. Suddenly the parent sat down and the discussion about organizing a parent group ceased. I seized the uniquely appropriate opportunity as a researcher to participate in the organization of the parent group. The situation was perfect because I had hypothesized that the issues and information which the Spanish-speaking parents raised relative to parent-school communication could be discussed among themselves, which could provide a support base for them to be able to deal more effectively with the school and thus break the isolation that many felt was a barrier.

After the meeting I approached the man who had made the suggestion and continued to discuss with him the possibility of getting a group of parents together to share his idea. I offered to meet with him and group of other parents. He suggested a few parents' names, but he said that he did not have their 'phone numbers. I asked him if he knew who might have them. He quickly turned to Mr Reyes, who was still in the room, and said, 'El señor Reyes tiene una lista. [Mr Reyes has a list.]' I felt a conflict between orchestrating for the purpose of research and really helping them for their own purposes.

Field Intervention and Ethics

Spradley (1979) has criticized ethnographers for their often removed and uninvolved position in the midst of a real life crisis. He suggests that ethnographers ethically cannot assume a totally distant position when the conditions dictate deliberate intervention. My intent in encouraging the parents to organize a leadership group stemmed from my systematic knowledge base about the isolating experiences which the parents had conveyed in their interviews. Furthermore, the organization of a group theoretically seemed an appropriate context in which to observe the development of parent involvement for Spanish-speakers and to understand the social and cultural knowledge required to participate in the school system. By assisting parents to organize themselves I would have access to the process of sociocultural change for these parents who intended to make an impact on the school system. Part of ethnography means continual analysis, which required the researcher to return to the field in search for further clarification of the data.

Clarification in regard to the position of the Migrant Program Director and the proposed leadership of the parent group is needed. The question was raised to the director about the role of administrators in the District in respect of parent groups. He commented that no one person in the district had charge of parent involvement except possibly, Mr Clark, the Director of Special Projects. According to Mr Reyes, each special program requiring parent involvement was supervised by its respective coordinator or principal. For example, in his Migrant Program he had jurisdiction on issues pertaining to the program over the parents whose children participate. He added that personnel in the District seemed quite overloaded with the administration of their programs and that the coordination of parent education for Spanish-speaking parents had been ignored except for the special program requirements. This information further confirmed my need to pursue the organization of parents as a systematic intervention in order to collect more data on the process of cultural change and to assist parents in this important process that could positively affect their relationship with their children and the schools.

Researcher's Role in Program Development

As the context changes, so does the researcher's role. My role as a researcher changed because I became involved in facilitating meetings with the parents who began to organize themselves. Given the data analysis on the family and parent education programs, I felt that I had sufficient data to understand that the parents needed some guidance in organizing themselves to participate in the schools. The criteria for intervention included the following description of my role as a researcher/advocate.

1 My knowledge of ways to assist the parents to organize their parent group was based largely on the information I had acquired during my research on the families' knowledge about the schools.

2 I saw my role as that of a facilitator who encouraged parents to generate their own knowledge and to validate it as they progressed in their organization. Part of the facilitator role also required a certain amount of direction on my part to ensure that the parents considered the various options they had. This could generally be accomplished by raising questions to the parents about the kind of decisions they needed to make as they proceeded.

3 The parents would be encouraged to initiate and take the lead role in calling meetings and making decisions about the direction they wanted to take. My role as facilitator would ensure that during the meetings the parents would explore the topics they had in mind and that they had the necessary information to make decisions. I would summarize their points and make suggestions to help move the discussion along. I would also provide them with data which I had collected to facilitate their decision-making.

4 I would act as a resource to the parents by sharing data which they requested on other parent education programs in California from which they could obtain ideas.

5 Initially in the process of organization I would become the liaison between the parents and the School District personnel. I would maintain constant communication with the Director of Special Projects and relate the progress of the group as well as suggesting ways in which the District could support the parents' efforts. In turn, the parents would be apprised of the District's interest in their group.

6 During the process of assisting the parents to organize their group, I would continue data collection procedures through fieldnotes, audio recordings and occasional videotaping to document the stages of parents' knowledge acquisition in relating to the schools.

My role as facilitator in the intervention would allow me to be both an advocate and a researcher. Although the two roles were often performed simultaneously due to the nature of the intervention, I kept notes on the process so that the parents' role could be reconstructed in the study.

Chapter 3

Home and School Linkages to Literacy

This chapter aims to integrate the three major parts of the Portillo study under one theoretical umbrella. The three parts are (1) the process of literacy acquisition at school; (2) the process of literacy acquisition at home; and (3) what parents are doing with other parents that relates to their ability to deal more effectively with text as well as with the social systems.

By the time children arrive at school they have both preconceptions and expectations about one another. Such perceptions are socially determined since schools are part of the community and the children's home-community experience has already prepared them in some way for schooling (Cook-Gumperz, 1986:7; De Castell, Luke and Egan, 1986; Erickson, 1984; Smith, 1986). The many assumptions that students, teachers and parents hold about the outcomes of schooling are culturally and socially determined. Literacy is one of those socially defined phenomena that is constructed through the process of schooling.

Literacy as discussed in much of the research has meant the ability to decode and construct symbols in order to read and write, generally for practical reasons such as academic achievement or obtaining employment. However, literacy extends beyond the skills of reading and writing. It involves the sociocultural context as it is relevant to the person involved. People's awareness of their sociopolitical environment, their participation in it, and the meaning they ascribe to it bear significantly on the process of becoming literate (Cook-Gumperz, 1986; Freire and Macedo, 1987; Gumperz, 1986). Freire's literacy work in Brazil's peasant communities and with other oppressed groups around the world shows the power of teaching people to participate in any given society by first teaching them to become conscious about their role and position in that society. From that basis people can decide how they want to change their situation. It is this process of understanding one's conditions and collectively working toward changing those conditions that empowers those involved in the process—a process not restricted to peasant communities. The social process of constructing reality and transmitting knowledge is inherent in the way in which children interact with their teachers in the classroom on a day-to-day basis and with their parents in the home (Gumperz, 1986). The process of literacy building, therefore, is significantly affected by how information is made available through the classroom curriculum, how skills are defined and cognitive abilities evaluated; that is, the form that knowledge takes and access to it are both socially defined and interactively constrained (Gumperz, 1986:68). Literacy is constructed through a process of tests and evaluations both standardized and informal; thus schooling is not just being able to do certain things, but knowing how to operate appropriately within a particular context. It follows that literacy is not only knowing how to read and write but also being able to utilize these skills in a socially appropriate context. This process of cultural transmission of knowledge applies not only to the teacher-student relationship but also to parent-child and parent-parent relationships. Literacy that incorporates people's competence in their social setting becomes a meaningful construct in its function to empower those involved (Cochran, 1987; Freire and Macedo, 1987). The concept of empowerment has numerous meanings. For the purposes of this study the most appropriate definition applies to the change which a person or a group of people undergoes that enables them to participate fully in their social environment. The change involved in empowerment is most often realized through interaction between people or between institutions. The process is best described by Cochran (1987:11) and Vanderslice (1984:2–3):

> an interactive process involving mutual respect and critical reflection through which both people and controlling institutions are changed in ways which provide those people with greater influence over individuals and institutions which are in some way impeding their efforts to achieve equal status in society, for themselves and those they care about. Furthermore, meaningful changes occur when people work together on behalf of something greater than themselves as individuals.

Literacy in and out of school can be understood within this concept of empowerment and helps us to explain how Mexican children learn to read in the classroom, how parents teach their children at home, and how parents and teachers communicate with each other about the children's schooling. All three of these areas fit into the equation of literacy and empowerment with social context interaction as the unifying dimension.

School literacy constitutes a wide range of classroom activities that have as their goal the acquisition of literacy skills. Here, however, we are most concerned with understanding the interaction that takes place within the social context of the literacy act. Central to this notion is the process of interaction between people in their environment rather than a measure of the products of interaction. The classroom reading lesson, for example, is an interaction context characterized by its participants. The context refers to the activity in which participants are engaged (Cole *et al.*, 1971; Erickson and Schultz, 1977; Gumperz, 1971). Theorists have argued that children can learn best in contexts in which language is culturally and linguistically meaningful (Cole and Griffin, 1983; Cole and D'Andrade, 1982; Scribner and Cole, 1981; Tharp and Gallimore, 1988; Vygotsky, 1978; Wertsch, 1985). Contexts are culturally defined by what, where and when people are doing something and what that activity means to them. In the study of students whose language is other than English, the focus is on language as part of the interaction, not as an abstract system (Diaz, Moll and Mehan, 1986:193). The context-interaction theory proposes that students and teachers organize to create a sequence of acts (Cole, 1981; Wertsch, 1981, 1985).

The study of family literacy requires an understanding of the culturally variable family education process (Heath, 1982; Leichter, 1979, 1984). Complex motives, symbols, categories and concepts organize the everyday life of a family relative to literacy. A crucial feature of families as educators is that much education in the home takes place on a moment-to-moment basis, including both those processes that are 'deliberate, systematic, and sustained' (Cremin, 1976, 1977) and those fleeting actions that take place at the margins of awareness (Leichter, 1974) cited in Leichter (1984:38).

Leichter (1979) states that while it may be argued that an educational curriculum or an educational agenda exists within families, the curriculum takes a different shape from that of the school in terms of space and time. Thus family literacy activities need to be understood in their own terms. Although formal educational activities, particularly homework, account for much of the frequent literacy activity in the homes of the twenty Portillo families in this study, informal instruction also plays a significant role. Leichter (1984) terms this literacy socialization within families and it provides an avenue to the knowledge which parents possess and share about their culture, and what they communicate to children in the way of language, cognitive skills and values.

Leichter (1984) utilized three general categories to define family events and ways in which parents act as educators. Parent educational attainment, parent-child interaction, and parental aspirations characterize the levels of interaction within the family. The first category suggests the inclusion of those activities influenced by parental education and family background. The problem with these three categories is the inherent overlap of the first with the third category of parental aspirations. Parents promote children's education through their emotional and material support systems, which are largely influenced by their own educational attainment and the knowledge involved in providing their children with the necessary material, psychological and cognitive resources. Leichter's work on parents as educators forces us to consider the natural learning environments in the home which directly or indirectly have an impact on children's schooling. This leads us to pose more specific questions about the social context of home-school relationships and the role of parents in relation to their children's schooling.

Parent involvement is the salient part of the literacy empowerment equation in this study, as Latino parents attempted to learn about the schooling system in the United States to help their children to achieve. The research literature on parent involvement is abundant but fragmented; to make the concept of parent involvement meaningful, we need to establish a framework in which to understand parental involvement in their children's education in terms of empowerment to participate.

In the early twentieth century chances existed for parents and schools to cooperate with each other or for conflicts to exist between the two (Waller, 1932). The characteristics of society at that time provided a much more authoritarian school system which largely ignored the diversity in class, gender and ethnicity which it now attempts to include (Comer, 1984; Lareau, 1987). Sociocultural mobility was extremely limited prior to social movements such as the civil rights movement, which challenged segregation issues, and the national women's movement, which opened opportunities for women in the labor force thus changing the character of the family and creating new responsibilities for schools. School reforms during the 1960s gave rise to more open classrooms and other educational innovations involving cooperation between teachers and parents. The parent involvement issue gave rise to research on childrearing in relation to children's learning processes in their sociocultural context.

Much of the research on children's learning in the family has been pejorative toward lower working-class and ethnic families by character-izing middle-class parents as more affectionate, responsible and effective in their parenting practices than working-class families (Coser, 1967). This perspective reflects a deficit hypothesis which has attributed learning differences of working-class minority group children to biological, cultural or economic factors (Dunn, 1987; Hess and Shipman, 1965; Holtzman, Diaz-Guerrero and Swartz, 1975). Laosa (1983) claims that much research on parent participation of Mexican American families has been limited to discussions of socialization and has relied on only a very few dimensions that became the undergirding factors for explaining Mexican American socialization, child development and parent involvement.

The general premise in these studies is that minority working-class families fail their children linguistically and cognitively by not providing them with the middle-class language and values which tend to prevail in middle-class mainstream families. This perspective on child development in the home is important to understanding the role of parents in their children's education because it may influence the school's view of and communication with parents. These deficit theory explanations fail to provide a holistic explanation of the family's sociocultural context and represent a context-bound unit of knowledge for understanding language, literacy and cognitive development.

Parent participation in their children's schooling takes many forms in the home and in the school depending on factors such as parents' knowledge of the school, their ability to communicate in the same language as that of the school, and the school's receptivity in involving parents. Research literature is replete with studies that indicate the overwhelming need for parents to become involved in their children's schooling because of the positive effects on student achievement (Becher, 1984; Leler, 1983; Goodson and Hess, 1975). Studies have shown that the manner in which parents organize natural learning environments in the home as part of their everyday lives (Leichter, 1979) enhances children's school achievement. Parent involvement research also describes ways in which parents become active in the school's governing bodies. These aspects of families' relationship with the school and their children's education reflect an expectation that parents play a decisive role in their children's schooling and education in general.

While many aspects of this issue have been studied, the question remains: why is it so important for parents to become involved in their children's schooling and how is knowledge about the school and ways to work with their children communicated to the parents? These considerations raise another issue that relates to schools' differential treatment of different social and cultural groups and their participation in school. The literature points to an overall positive effect of parents' involvement in their children's schooling, but there is little research to explain and describe the process that parents undergo in participating in the school. The three major categories presented here outline the research on different levels of parent involvement. They describe the undergirding theoretical assumptions in children's schooling.

While no single theory explains the role of Spanish-speaking parents in their children's literacy acquisition and overall participation in schools, the research reviewed in this chapter explores the involvement of parents in their children's schooling and what that involvement means to the schools, parents and children. Much of the research on parent involvement is represented in three models that describe the nature and outcomes of parent involvement. The family influence model describes research in which the school has attempted to change home life for it to fit the values of the school. The school reform model reports research on parents attempting to change the school through participation in advisory committees. The cooperative systems model, which extends beyond research presented in the previous two models, involves parents in the educational system in various ways from attending workshops to being employed in the schools. The model shows the levels of progressive involvement on the part of the parents and the schools. All the research in these models shows positive results in some way in that they try to educate parents to help their children in a variety of ways. The models explicate more fully the type of involvement and its significance to empowerment of families relative to the schools.

Research on Three Levels of Parent Involvement

Family Influence Model

The family influence model encompasses research on methods to improve the family's capabilities in helping their children learn and to provide the type of home learning environment that accentuates the positive elements of cognitive and emotional factors. Research by Gordon (1978) and Coleman (1966) indicates that the home environment accounts for almost 50 per cent of variations in children's school achievement. However, many parent education efforts in this model have operated on the 'deficit view of the family'. The assumptions here, according to Gordon (1978), are that a body of information exists that is essential for life, that teachers know and teach it, and that individuals, including parents, learn and apply it. This premise assumes that the right way to rear children can be learned from books or experts, and that parents who apply this information can be successful in their role as parents. Home learning environments and implications for schooling are the focus of such research.

The study of the role of the home in children's schooling must reject notions such as those proposed by Coleman that differences in achievement are not due to the school's curriculum and instruction, but rather to the family background. According to Coleman (1987), a strong background will yield higher achievement regardless of the nature of the school. Furthermore, he claimed that parental inattention in this country is the reason for children's low achievement scores. This position reveals an unsubstantiated simple cause for an extremely complex problem. This perspective is expanded here by assuming a broader definition of the family and its role in children's education. Coleman is remiss in not accounting for the role of schools or for the role of culture and socioeconomic status, which clearly have an impact on educational outcomes.

A more appropriate account of the role of the family in children's achievement attempts to understand how the family functions as an environment for learning. The home environment has been identified as the primary learning environment, particularly in early childhood (Comer, 1984). According to Comer, parents and extended family networks guide children through increasingly complex intellectual tasks, and this is facilitated through the attachment process. Children internalize the experiences of the household as they develop a sense of belonging, worth and identity.

Research on family environments has focused to a large extent on literacy acquisition (Leichter, 1984). Environments condition children for literacy through the physical setting, the level of economics and the parents' resources. To understand family literacy it has been necessary to understand the culturally variable family education process (Leichter, 1974, 1984). This requires an understanding of the motives, symbols and concepts that organize the everyday life of a family relative to literacy. A crucial feature of families as educators in the home, noted by Cremin (1976, 1977), Leichter (1974, 1979), McDermott, Goldman and Varenne (1984), is that much education takes place on a moment-to-moment basis, including those processes that are deliberate, systematic and sustained.

Education in the home is influenced by characteristics such as education and income levels of the parents. Family behaviors, such as whether parents read to children and enforce rules about homework and television, also shape the home learning environment. Family patterns, marital status, employment, social support network all help to explain the family's ability to relate to the school. Furthermore, family attitudes, such as parental expectations and the child's self esteem, provide an emotional framework for the children's home learning environment.

Generally studies that focus on home environments measure the effects in terms of school performance (Albert and Runco, 1985; Bloom, 1985). The home setting of a variety of age-groups has been examined to learn how parents engage in supportive activities in the home. These studies have found that creating a positive learning environment at home, including encouraging attitudes toward education and high expectations of children's success, has a powerful impact on student achievement. These unsurprising results reveal that the more academically successful students most often come from families where the parents are enthusiastically involved in every aspect of their development.

Albert and Runco (1985) conducted a longitudinal study of two groups of gifted 12-year-old boys. They found that the parents' creative activities in the home related to the boys' creative achievement. Parents discussed television programs, reading materials, homework, and initiated hobby activities with the children.

Comparable conclusions were reached by Bloom (1985), whose case study consisted of twenty young talented professionals (ages 28–35), whose fields included tennis, mathematics, classical piano and neurology. In each case the young professionals exceeded their parents' expertise. They noted, however, that even after they had surpassed their parents' accomplishments, they continued to receive enthusiasm and encouragement which conveyed confidence and trust.

Different conditions were found in homes whose children were said to be 'at risk' academically. These children usually excelled in school once their parents received training in the home teaching techniques (Boulder Valley, Colorado School District, 1975; Bronfenbrenner, 1974a, 1974b; Gotts, 1980; Lazar and Darlington, 1978; Scott and Davis, 1979). As children begin to experience difficulty in school, parent education techniques to assist children at home yielded rewarding results for the children (Karraker, 1972).

The preschool family intervention programs were shown to have positive effects by Bronfenbrenner (1974a), who studied mothers who received training in how to stimulate verbal interaction with their children. Long-lasting gains were made in a two-year program where tutors visited homes twice a week and demonstrated toy kits to mothers and children. Less frequent sessions or training just for mothers were found to be less effective.

An experimental study in the Boulder Valley, Colorado, School District (1975) documented that academically high risk kindergarten children in the experimental group scored higher on standardized tests when their parents received teacher-designed, parent-child home training than did high risk children in the control group who participated only in an in-school enhancement program. This study revealed longer-lasting effects on first grade tests for children whose parents had received both school and home training on specific enrichment activities.

A long-term study of eleven early childhood projects (Lazar and Darlington, 1978) confirmed the long-term effects on children of parents who actively participated in their preschool education. They had significantly fewer assignments to special education and fewer grade retentions than the control group. Although parent involvement was not isolated and separately measured as a factor in program effectiveness, largely because there was substantial parent involvement in all the programs studied, the researchers believed that it was an integral part of a cluster of factors essential to program success. It was near the top of the list as fundamental to program effectiveness.

A long-term study of the effects of a three-year preschool enrichment program centered in the homes of eighty-nine children in Waterloo, Iowa. Older siblings of forty-four members of the experimental group served as a control group. Paraprofessional home-school liaison workers met once a week with mothers or guardians to hold family-like conversations about family interactions, the child's activities and the types of books and toys that were available from the program's library. All the children attended an enrichment program for one year for two and a half hours a day to familiarize them with materials and conversational strategies which the students would be likely to encounter in kindergarten. Using the Learning Reading System Seriation Test in the preschool program's last year and the Iowa Test of Basic Skills when the students reached the third grade, Scott and Davis (1979) found significant gains for the Black children but not for the White children in the experimental group. The total group, however, averaged equivalencies that were one year higher than their older siblings.

In 1980 Gotts examined longitudinal effects (five-year) on Appalachian preschool children aged 3–5 whose parents had been trained in their home on a weekly visit by paraprofessionals to augment daily lessons broadcast on television. This experimental group showed consistently higher achievement on the Appalachian Preschool Test, the Frostig Test of Visual Perception and the Peabody Picture Vocabulary Test through the first five years of their school careers than the control group children who received only television lessons without augmented activities. With the home visits/parents home training as the single variable, the children's first follow-up showed children in the experimental group achieving higher grade point averages on higher basic skills test scores and higher attendance figures than did the control counterparts. Similar findings surfaced in the second follow-up when students were tested with emotional development instruments.

The reasons for children's success in school are not as simple as they are depicted in the research discussed, especially in the single factor studies. Certainly children perform better in school if they have extra attention and help, but the research on home interventions showed lasting academic gains for children whose parents were trained by school-related personnel in their own home to assist the students. The difference is that students' attitudes about themselves and their control over their environment are critical to achievement (Bronfenbrenner, 1979b; Tizard, Scholfield and Hewison, 1982). When parents show interest in their children's learning (which is congruent with the expectations of the school), children's academic performance usually increases. These studies stress that parents must encourage their children to talk about books they read, to converse with their children about school and to practice school-like curriculum including colors, letters and math concepts.

While the intention to have children achieve in school through supportive family environments presents an honorable enough intent, what is absent in these studies is any insight about family organizational structures. That is, most of the studies declared academic success to be a critical factor in children's school achievement, a point that has been well substantiated, but most assumed that what parents may be doing in the home is insufficient to meet the school's demands in helping children achieve. Such deficiencies are presumed to be corrected by school-designed interventions that make home socialization congruent with the school culture. In these studies, teaching parents how to talk with their children in the language of the school became the school's way of remedying the children's achievement problem.

Inherent in this research is the failure to examine and to view the family's sociocultural environment in the home and to understand it as a source of knowledge about the children which could be used in the classroom. The message in this research could be that the school needs to have the family reflect the school's culture regardless of the family's own experience and the source of information that it could provide about the children for the school. Clark (1983) concludes in his case study of ten Black high school students and their families that a family's overall cultural style, not marital status, educational level, income or social surroundings, determines whether children are prepared for competent performance in school.

Clark (1983) and McDermott *et al.* (1984) overcome the obvious neglect of many other researchers in representing the integrity of the family's home learning environment, which Leichter (1974, 1984) concludes to be an essential element in the study of families as educators. A compelling point in this type of research is the recognition that home environments are critical to children's achievement through the attitudes and interactions between parents and children in the home. Cochran and Henderson (1986) and Revicki (1981) believe that part of parent involvement implies congruent home and school learning environments through school-designed interventions. That is, not only is the family influenced by the school, but the school is also influenced by the family.

McDermott *et al.* (1984) discuss still another angle of the relationship of home learning environments and school in their ethnographic study of two families. The authors were concerned with literacy events that parents pass on to children. They recognized that informal learning goes on in the home. This learning is unstructured and fits in with the flow of life. However, school situations can be recreated in the home, especially in homework activities when parents assume a formal teacher role. Motivation, skill and achievement preoccupy the participants during homework. The authors suggest that assignments be personalized to fit the child's particular familial environment. An example would be learning the value of literacy by 'freeing' students from the burden of homework and letting them enjoy a good story.

The family influence model seems to encompass research that views the family as a direct recipient of the school's influence and as a mutual collaborator in establishing effective environments for learning. The fact that home interventions described in much of the research succeed in influencing the family cannot be challenged. This raises questions about the parents' role in their children's schooling beyond the domain of the home.

School Reform Model

The school reform model includes research that shows how family and school influence shifts from the home to the school. In this model parents may try to change the schools to make them more responsive to parents. The hope is that if educators become more attuned to the family and the culture of the home, they can teach and serve the child more effectively. In this model, according to Gordon (1978) and Leler (1983), parent involvement means parent participation in the classroom and the school, as well as serving on policy or advisory councils. The parents learn to deal with schools, and the goal is to change those institutions and make them more responsive to student and family needs in a way that would lead to greater educational achievement for children. The assumption is that the school will accommodate the parents' suggestions and influence. Research on parent contact with schools is the focus of this section.

The need for interconnectedness of family, school and other community agencies is the focus of research by McGuire and Lyons (1985), who found that most children referred to mental health services experience school-related problems and underachievement. The authors state that psychotherapy in itself is ineffective in reducing achievement problems because of the influence of such variables as parental skills in child management and school practices. The solutions to under-achievement in cases that were referred to therapy, argue McGuire and Lyons (1985), lie in interventions which can promote family negotiations with the school.

Becher (1984) in a review of research, found that in school-based programs where low socioeconomic parents have been trained to work with their children significant academic improvement on the part of the students ensued.

Parent involvement components in the schools have been studied (Gordon, 1978; Herman and Yeh, 1980; Irvine, 1979) to understand parents' impact on the school and indirectly on their children's achievement. Research has concluded that in parent intervention programs for preschool programs, children whose families participated actively do better in school than comparable children whose parents did not participate. The effects have been studied for as long as ten years after the children left the preschool program. Parent impact on programs for school-aged children, however, has not been as thoroughly researched (Gordon, 1978). Thus it is more difficult to determine the nature of programs that promote parent–teacher contact. The limited research available, for example, on programs such as the Follow Through Program provides a good example of high student, school and community impact. The Follow Through Program is a national effort designed to have counselors based at an institution of higher education to assist junior high and high school students through daily tutoring. Summer intensive courses, family resources and counseling are also provided. Gordon shows that the more comprehensive and long-lasting the parent involvement activities, the more likely the effectiveness. The effects surpass the students' achievement by affecting the quality of the schools serving the community.

An experimental study by Irvine (1979) showed that the amount of time spent by parents of low working-class preschool children in New York was related to student achievement. Parent involvement included school visits, home visits by school personnel, meetings, employment in the program and incidental contacts. The researcher controlled for factors such as level of family education, children's age, previous performance and family income to determine the precise effect of parent involvement. Four levels of involvement were determined according to the number of hours (50, 100, 150, 200 hours) the parents were involved over the school year. School-related knowledge and skills as measured by the Cooperative Preschool Inventory and the Peabody Picture Vocabulary Test showed a highly significant relationship between parent involvement and achievement, with the greatest gains made by children who initially had the lowest scores.

Herman and Yeh (1980) studied parent involvement in 250 California elementary preschool programs and found a positive connection between student achievement and parent satisfaction with the school. The categories involved were school-home communication, parent awareness of school operations, parent influence, parent participation in school functions and activities, and parent-teacher relations. The correlation study showed significant relationships between parent participation in school activities and student achievement; between decision-making involvement of parents in the school and good parent teacher relationships, and between parent involvement and satisfaction. Thus parent involvement, according to Herman and Yeh, seemed imperative for student achievement and parent satisfaction with the school.

Epstein (1987) concluded that students gain in personal and academic development if their families emphasize schooling in every way possible during the students' school career. She conducted a survey study of longitudinal data of 293 third and fifth grade students who took the California Achievement Test (CAT) in the fall and spring of the 1980-81 school year. The students were divided among fourteen teachers who varied in their emphasis on parental involvement. They were classified by themselves and their principals as frequent users of parent involvement, infrequent users and non-users of parent involvement. Findings from the pre- and post-test scores for that year showed that teacher leadership toward parent involvement in home literacy activities positively and significantly influenced change in school reading achievement scores. Furthermore, children of parents who reported that they had learned more ways to help their children showed positive effects on reading achievement, as did children of parents with higher educational background who received help at home.

Generally research has demonstrated that parents were the basic ingredient in a strong academic program for all students and particularly in the case of children and families from the working classes. Although studies clearly showed positive effects of parent-teacher contact, most of the research focused on the children's academic gains rather than on the ways in which parents learned how to become more involved and the kind of changes observed in addition to children's test scores. A great deal remains unknown as to the particular way in which parents learn how to become involved.

Research by Lareau (1987) indicates that middle-class family-school relationships differ somewhat from those of working-class families. The difference shows that although parents of both middle- and working-class families share a desire for their children's educational success, the family's social location leads them to construct different pathways for realizing that success. Parents approach the family–school relationship with different sets of social resources. Schools ask for very similar types of behavior from all parents, regardless of their social class, and not all cultural resources are equally valuable for complying with schools' requests (Lareau, 1987:83). The resources tied directly to social class, such as education, prestige, income, certain patterns of family kinship and leisure activities, seem to play a large role in facilitating parent participation in schools. This supports the notion of examining parent involvement in working-class minority parents from a more holistic perspective in order to understand the specific process that would yield more effective family–school relations.

Cooperative Systems Model

In the cooperative systems model it is expected that the influence goes to and from home, school and the larger community to include the parents' employment as paraprofessionals in the school. The assumption is that factors in the home, school and community are interrelated. Furthermore, it is assumed that cooperation between the two institutions of the family and the school exists. In this process parents should play six roles: volunteer, paid employee, teacher at home, audience, decision-maker, adult learner. For parents and schools to have a relationship based on mutual involvement, parents must play all of these roles. Here the assumption is that parent education needs to be concerned not only with 'how to' questions but with strategic issues of how parent involvement fits into the larger social scheme, including the parents' employment opportunities and their social position.

Warren (1988) reported on his study of three communities with distinctively different characteristics or settings: a village in rural, southwest Germany, an Anglo middle-class neighborhood in a northern Californian metropolis, and a lower-class Mexican American neighborhood in a southern Californian metropolis. Parents and teachers played a key role in the children's socialization. The structural characteristics which these schools had in common significantly overshadowed the cultural differences. The striking common feature of the three schools was the absence of an effective bond between parents and teachers. In all three communities relations between parents and teachers were complex, tentative and stressful. Warren points to the need for both sides to accommodate to each other in an effort to provide children with the instruction and support they require.

Other researchers have also studied the characteristics of comprehensive parental involvement programs. The Follow Through (FT) programs have had a long tradition of affecting achievement through a comprehensive community model involving the family, the institutions and the students. Washington, DC School District showed positive effects on achievement in an elementary school program serving low income students in a segregated setting studied by Gross, Ridgley and Gross (1974). A comprehensive development program for staff, parents and community included community development as well as in-service programs for the staff. Parents were trained through workshops and continuing education classes such as health and consumer education. Parents also attended family counseling services weekly. Teachers, on the other hand, held monthly discussions on professional topics including report cards, individualized instruction, achievement testing and parent-teacher sharing. Teachers were also given time to observe other classrooms and to attend conferences and in-service training sessions. The overall evaluation of the parent and teacher and community efforts to improve the educational program showed an increase in the number of parents receiving credit toward their high school diploma, or General Education Development certificate (GED), the number of persons referred for community services and the number of parents involved in the total school program (Gross, Ridgley and Gross, 1974, cited in Leler, 1983:171).

Another program, 'Training Migrant Paraprofessionals in Bilingual Mini Head Start', has been studied for its efforts to train the families in the program. Eighty families participated in McConnell's studies (1976, 1979). McConnell described the program as bilingual multicultural education for children from preschool through third grade. All were children of migrant and seasonal farm workers. By working cooperatively with the public schools which the children attended, the mobile project staff arranged sessions with the children on released time from their regular classes or after school, to provide supplementary education in math, reading, bilingual skills and cultural concepts and activities (McConnell, 1976:169).

Decision-making for this program included parents as well as community members through an organized parent/community advisory group in the three sites (two in Washington and one in Texas) where the specific Migrant Training programs were located. Frequent general meetings were held where parents decided on issues including budgetary decisions, organizational matters, personnel actions, planning for funding proposals, discussion of the educational program and program evaluation. Family members acted as teacher assistants and helped out with cultural heritage activities and other support services (McConnell, 1976:169–70). The research findings showed student achievement gains in math and reading. Kindergarten achievement was above that of other Spanish-speaking migrant counterparts in Texas, while 83 per cent improved in bilingual capability. The parents' involvement accounted for much of the students' academic success.

The importance of parental involvement in federally funded educational programs was described in a 1980 national study headed by Melaragno, Keesling, Lyons, Robbins and Smith. This was a major three-year study which involved four federal programs, ESEA, Title VII, Upward Bound, and Title I. The four programs differed not only in intent and populations served, but also in the regulated role of parental involvement. While there were differences in the legislation and guidelines, all four programs required the creation of some form of advisory council consisting of community members including parents of children served by the programs.

Two stages of the study provided a comprehensive examination of parental involvement in the four federal programs across the nation through survey and descriptive techniques. The study completed six major tasks: (1) it described parental involvement in the four programs; (2) it identified factors that facilitated or inhibited parental involvement; (3) it determined the consequences of parental involvement; (4) it specified models of parental involvement; (5) is disseminated findings; and (6) it validated the models of parental involvement. The findings indicated that parents involved themselves in project governance, as paid para-professionals, as volunteers and as teachers of their own children.

The major conclusion of this study was that legislation and regulation can provide a powerful motivation to foster and support parental involvement. The data support the fact that differences among programs in the nature and extent of parental involvement are related to differences in legislation and regulations defining the programs. Secondary findings showed that the level of funding influenced the extent of parental involvement, as well as the importance of monitoring the extent to which districts implement mandated activities. Within the context of each of the national programs, the value of emphasizing parental involvement has to be weighed against the value assigned to other components demanding support, especially the provision of instructional services. The study indicated that the level of parental involvement could be increased if: (1) the legislation provided incentives for involvement; (2) funding was provided for specific activities; and (3) some form of monitoring the implementation of specified activities was provided. Findings showed that the parents, more than any other group of individuals, were more consistently and positively affected by their own involvement in project activities. Through direct participation they gained more knowledge of the opportunities that were available to them and of their potential importance to the school's goals. Findings also raised issues of how more meaningful involvement of parents in school activities can be achieved in order to increase the frequency of positive effects of such involvement.

A group of Cornell University professors, Bronfenbrenner, Cross and Cochran, studied the capacity of urban American environments to serve as support systems to parents and other adults directly involved in the care, upbringing and education of children (Bronfenbrenner, 1979a). The significance of the Cornell Family Matters Program study, as well as other studies cited here raises a fundamental question about the meaning of parental involvement as it relates to children's education. The study involved 276 families in the city of Syracuse, New York. All families had a 3-year-old child. The families were distributed evenly among eighteen Syracuse neighborhoods, and family incomes ranged between low working-class and upper middle-class groups. One-third of the families were Black and one-third were single parent families.

The five-year project assumed an ecological perspective to explain the influences of growth which were defined as a series of encounters across, as well as within, the ecological system. Families were involved in program activities for twenty-six months, and the program terminated the summer prior to the children's first grade entry. The home- and family-focused strategy took the form of home visits with parents and their children designed to give recognition to the parenting role, to reinforce and enrich parent-child activities and to share information about child care and community services. Paraprofessionals hired from the Syracuse community were trained to exchange information about childrearing with parents and, when appropriate, to provide examples of parent-child activities geared to the developmental age of the child. The starting point was to establish the level of expertise that parents possessed about their own children, and so early home visits were spent learning parents' views of the child and seeking examples of activities that were already being carried out with the child and defined by the parent as important to the child's development (Cochran, 1987:15). The paraprofessional workers attempted to value the parental point of view, they identified a wide variety of activities that parents engaged in with their children and which they felt made a difference to both the parent and the child. Activities were shared with other families in a process of understanding parental stresses and support. One finding was that empowerment was a process rather than an end and that it occurred over time. Parents who initially viewed themselves negatively began to believe in themselves through this process. Thus the program influenced parental perceptions. Ultimately the families received individual attention from the Family Matters workers, and individual families experienced positive gains from the program in terms of their ability to change day-to-day practices and attitudes. However, the program failed to stimulate collective organization on the part of the parents. This could have enabled them to change the balance of power between the families and the schools and other institutions (Barr *et al.*, 1984; Cochran, 1987).

The Meaning of Parent Involvement

The issue of parental involvement has often been dichotomized either in the home or school but research cannot ignore the integral relationship between the two. One cannot be examined in isolation from the other. Beyond the home learning setting, the extent to which parents become involved in various aspects of their children's formal education has an impact on the level of academic achievement. Although much parental involvement in the school is more intense in preschool and early childhood years, it has been noted that parent involvement is most effective when it is systematic, consistent and protracted. Responsibility rests with both the family and the school to create and maintain this relationship. Most studies on parent involvement have focused largely on white middle-class groups, while those focusing on working-class and minority groups clearly show that these groups stand to benefit more from school when parents are involved (Campos and Keatinge, 1988).

Research reveals that the family provides the most essential educational environment for children. Most of the studies aimed to teach parents how to work with their children in ways congruent with the school. Effectiveness was measured by the outcomes on the students' standardized test scores. While these strategies showed achievement gains for children, it is critical to examine the problem of parental involvement somewhat differently in relation to working-class minority families. Issues of language and cultural congruency, as well as total involvement in the process of developing effective parent education programs, need to be at the forefront of the parent involvement agenda for this group. The extent to which institutions perceive their role as empowering parents was discussed in the Syracuse study and revealed the value to families of learning from their day-to-day cultural tasks and sharing them with each other through an intermediary. The missing feature in the study was the collective organization of the parents, which could provide face-to-face interaction between parents and the target institutions through which they could negotiate power relations. It is this process of learning about the system by participating in it that we come to understand in the Portillo study.

The purpose of parent involvement must be seen beyond an increase in test scores, as important as that may be. Minority families, especially those from immigrant groups who have not been schooled in this country, face a complex set of problems in relating to school. Although research has shown that parents may learn specific school strategies to work with their children in the home and to intervene in the school through parent-teacher conferences and open house events, the school-designed programs may constrain parents to specific tasks in the home or the school. Because they are not involved in the more complete process of schooling, the social isolation of these families is perpetuated by restricting them to prescribed activities without an opportunity for more active participation in their children's schooling in other areas. Children's achievement and test scores are but one measure of schooling, and performance on such tests varies at many points of the students' school career. For this reason it should not be the sole purpose of encouraging parent involvement and developing parent education programs.

Parents have to deal with their children's schooling long past preschool and early grades. That is, parents may be trained to work with their children on specific tasks during the first years of schooling which yield positive results for their children during that period. What happens when the children move into more complex academic work or have homework that is only in English, as in the case of limited-English-speaking students? Consistent with the cooperative systems model, the parents need to understand not only how to help their children with specific tasks in the early years but also to understand how the school system functions so that they can continue to help their children as they move through the grades.

It is not efficient for children, parents or the school to view parent involvement as a discrete set of activities that satisfy federal mandates or teach a specific assistance skill. The most important skills which the schools need to help parents acquire are those of social competence and social literacy. These concepts extend beyond discrete tasks. It is important to consider the need for parents to work collectively with each other and the school to learn the meaning of parent involvement by becoming literate about the culture of the school, including the classroom curriculum, and how resources are accessed. As part of the cooperative systems equation, the school also needs to learn about the families it serves. The more the school recognizes and values the children's home culture in its curriculum and its communication with parents, the more effective home-school communication will be. This model presumes a highly interactive context between parents and children, teachers and students, teachers and parents, and parents and parents. Through collective effort parents can learn to act as advocates for their children beyond the homework level Thus they stand a better chance of providing their children with necessary resources as they move through the grades and of providing nurturing learning environments at home, even if the home language and culture differ from that of the school.

Many questions remain unanswered in the area of involvement of minority parents who speak a language other than English in the home. Most importantly, research needs to focus on the meaning of minority parent involvement in children's education given the family's generational tenure in the United States and sociocultural changes that occur in the family as parents learn to participate in their children's education. Research on involvement as it is revealed in day-to-day social interactions between teachers, students and parents is important.

Summary

If one examines the complexity of parent involvement from a literacy and empowerment perspective, various assumptions must be made to contextualize the issues of literacy in the school between teachers and students, in the home between parents and their children, and in the community between parent and educators. Four major theoretical assumptions guided the goals, design and analysis of the Portillo study:

1 First, all families have strengths (Bronfenbrenner, 1979a; Cochran and Woolever, 1983). Mexican American families demonstrate rich cultural experience and practices, contrary to the belief that they are culturally deficient (Laosa, 1982). Different forms of child rearing are legitimate and all can promote the development of high achieving students to the extent that parents can marshal resources to help to school their children. Such practices are sociocultural skills which are learned through 'mediating structures', including the family, school, church and community at large (Berger and Neuhaus, 1977; Lamb, 1976). Furthermore, if empowered through policy, these structures will empower the individual.

2 Literacy is a process not only of building skill but also of developing social competence through interaction with text in context with others. The context-specific approach assumes that literacy development is possible only if a person participates in

culturally meaningful activities in its acquisition (Cole *et al.*, 1971; Freire and Macedo, 1987; Diaz, Moll and Mehan, 1986; Trueba, 1989; Wertsch, 1985).

3 Social interaction is a vehicle in helping to understand the sociocultural learning process. Day-to-day social activity is the culture that embodies the meaning which individuals create through social interactions (Trueba, 1989; Wertsch, 1981, 1985).

4 Changes in the home pertaining to schooling cannot be made without the school's cooperation. Therefore, the role of school advocates who value minority students' language and culture needs to be examined as it effects the empowerment process for families (Cochran, 1987; Cummins, 1986; Freire and Macedo, 1987).

Literacy and empowerment presume that both the school and the home are responsible for the sociocultural changes required to benefit children's academic progress in school. The relationship between families and schools provides one perspective for understanding how Spanish-speaking people learn to participate more fully in society by participating in their children's schooling. The chapters that follow describe literacy and empowerment in Portillo by presenting the children in their classroom reading lessons and in interaction with their teachers. Next the home literacy-related activities, as well as homework and parental communication with the school, are considered. Finally, we see the parents take charge and organize through rigorous parent-parent interaction, and this leads to a new way of communicating and negotiating with the schools.

Chapter 4

Classroom Literacy Activities

In this chapter we observe the twenty children in the study in their second and third grade classroom literacy activities. The context-interaction theoretical model, based on the work of Diaz, Moll and Mehan (1986) and Cole *et al.* (1971), provided a framework for analyzing the discourse observed. The research was designed to discover how classroom literacy instruction was organized and how the students participated in that structure. As applied to classroom literacy instruction in this study, the concept of context-interaction consists of a sequence of teacher-student interactions and the student's written product. In essence, the context-interaction theory holds that language and thinking skills are used to promote higher order mental operations and meaningful comprehension of text through student-teacher interaction.

Teacher-student interaction and student written texts constitute the classroom literacy activity. The interrelationship of the acts is the basis of the context-interaction approach proposed by Diaz, Moll and Mehan (1986), Cole *et al.* (1971), Tharp and Gallimore (1987) and others, including Delgado-Gaitan (1989a), McDermott and Roth (1979), Moll and Diaz (1987) and Trueba (1984). As defined by Diaz, Moll and Mehan, the classroom literacy activity provides the opportunity for learning to occur.

In most cases, particularly in the classroom, these interactions consist of communications between people for the specific purpose of problem solving. In addition, the activity we call learning or problem solving always involves the achievement of many partial goals that require joint activity by teacher and students. Each of these goals, in turn, is reached by performing some act (Leont'ev, 1973; Talyzina, 1978). Hence, in the study of any learning activity, the unit of analysis becomes the act or system of acts by which learning is composed, as seen in the context of the classroom, the school, and the community. Consequently, a critical task in the analysis of educational interactions becomes the careful and detailed description of the learning activity (e.g., a reading lesson) and its constituent sequence of acts. These sequences of acts are jointly produced or collaboratively assembled by the teacher and students. Some sequences include the initiation of questioning by the teacher, the complementary answering of questions by the students, and the distribution and use of educational materials (Diaz, Moll and Mehan, 1986:191–2).

In the home parents interact with their children in homework literacy activities and attempt to recreate a school imposed activity often without the required skills. This chapter presents a perspective on the way in which teachers conduct formal literacy instruction in the classroom.

Literacy in the Classroom

Students and Teachers

Twenty Mexican, Spanish-speaking second and third grade students were the main participants in this part of the study. They represented a cross-section of literacy achievement in this second grade classroom. Marina elementary school was selected as the research site because of its bilingual program. The second and third grade levels allowed us to examine literacy instruction in the primary language, since typically after the second grade many Spanish-speaking students were moved into English literacy instruction. The advanced reading groups in Spanish scored at the mean of 79 per cent in the Spanish CTBS, while the mean score for the novice readers was 30 per cent. The students in novice reading groups read a full year below their grade level.

Literacy in Mrs Mata's Second Grade

Mrs Mata was the second grade teacher in Marina elementary school. She had taught for three years since receiving her credential. She was trained in a bilingual teacher education program which taught the use of the teacher's manual as the primary vehicle for literacy instruction. The emphasis in the literacy activity was on structure and management through the teacher's formulaic dialogue with the students about the text. At the time of the study the reading materials at Marina school were out of date, but the bilingual teachers had been unsuccessful in convincing the principal to purchase newer ones. Mrs Mata believed that literacy was the most important subject for the students: 'They need to learn language, reading and writing, otherwise they won't be able to do anything in this country.' Despite the limited resources and materials for Spanish-speaking students, Mrs Mata believed that she was doing the best she could.

Mrs Mata believed that her job was even more difficult than most because the parents of the Spanish-speaking students could not help their children to read since they did not know how to read, they worked long hours and were too tired. The teacher believed that the underachievement problem resulted from a lack of parental reinforcement of classroom teaching. She had to be very strict with the Mexican students because that was the best way for them to 'catch up'. The belief was that the students were generally farther behind in most skills than their Anglo mainstream counterparts.

In her classroom Mrs Mata placed the twenty-nine students in differential skill reading groups of novice (two groups), average (one group) and advanced (two groups). Two students (not in any group) were English-speakers and read at grade level. The teacher assistant usually worked with them on tasks similar to those of the Spanish-speaking students, except in English. Two other students who were Spanish-speaking worked individually because they were non-readers. They usually performed letter matching tasks until the teacher or the teacher assistant could work with them on the alphabet. Many of the tasks required the students to color the picture after underlining the correct beginning letter. Mrs Mata believed that the group of novice readers needed to memorize more vocabulary because they did not know as many words as the advanced group. The problem with the novice readers was that they did not remember what was in the story after they read it. The higher groups did not have that problem.

Mrs Mata also believed, as did the School District administration, that Spanish-speaking students should be taught to read in their first language until they learned English well enough to read fluently. There were two groups each of novice and advanced readers. Both groups at each level read the same book. The teacher separated the advanced and novice readers into two groups simply for management purposes.

Novice Reading Group

Ability groups were formed for children in the novice and advanced reading ability levels (see Table 5 for the composition of second grade

Table 5   Composition of Second Grade Reading Groups

	Advanced group	Novice group
1	Vivian Alonzo	Rita Dominguez
2	Maria Sanchez	Veto Solis
3	Juana Sandoval	Marco Toledo
4	Nano Barra	
5	Rafael Muños	

groups). Daily classroom reading lessons for the novice reading group were similar to those of the higher reading groups. Literacy activity occurred throughout the school day. Reading was taught during the first and last hours of the day. The teacher usually stood or sat in front of the group and told the students what the focus of the lesson was. For several weeks the focus for all reading groups was the 'point of the story'. Before students began to read, the teacher would tell them that they should read for the 'point of the story'. The students were first drilled in any new vocabulary in the story. The teacher flashed the new words and called on different students individually to read a word.

Following the initial vocabulary exercise (approximately fifteen words), the teacher asked the students to read and then answer two specific questions which would help discover the point of the story. The students were left to read individually and silently. Twenty minutes were usually allowed for students to read the assigned number of pages. The teacher usually began discussion about the text by calling on students who sat around the table. The entire presentation was conducted in Spanish. Literacy and math instruction was provided in Spanish until students learned English well enough to perform at grade level in their second language. If it was a long story, students were asked to read it during one class period and then discuss it with the teacher the following day. The following transcription represents a typical literacy activity for a novice reading group.

> (Mrs Mata met with the three students in this novice reading group. The two boys, Veto and Marco, sat next to each other apart from Rita, the only girl in the group. The teacher began the lesson by giving the children a spelling test on the vocabulary words unrelated to the story in the book. Each student had a spelling packet of word lists which they studied each week for a test. Mrs Mata dictated seven words and the students wrote them and passed their lists to the person on their right to correct. The teacher called on students to spell each of the words written on the board. Rita had her hand

up to spell a few of the words, but the teacher tended to call on the boys. After correcting the tests, the teacher left the group for about two minutes to give directions to another group. This group talked to each other about the number of words on the test that they each had right and wrong. Rita could not understand Veto's handwriting and complained to the teacher. Mrs Mata responded:)

T: Si no se entiende sus palabras, están mál. Tienen que estar escritas en letra bonita. [If you do not understand her words, they are wrong. They have to be written in clear form.]
(The children raised their hands if they received 100 per cent on their test. Rita and Marco received a star on the corner of the front page of their spelling packets.)

T: Las que sacaron mal, en sus asientos, escríbanlas diez veces. [At your seats write ten times those words you got wrong.]
(The teacher moved on to drill the children in vocabulary words related to the story in their reading book. When the word 'Kate' came up, Mrs Mata stopped and explained to the students about the word.)

T: 'Kate' es una palabra en inglés. Tienen [ustedes] que decir Kate en inglés cuando la ven. [Kate is a word in English. You have to say Kate in English when you see it.]
(Rita had her hand up for almost every one of the ten words, but the teacher seemed to call only on the boys. She recognized Rita for the last word. Mrs Mata also kept an eye on the two boys who sat next to each other and seemed to be paying attention to each other and not to the word drill. She moved Marco to the other side of Rita so that she was in the middle. The boys were told that they were not to sit together when they came to reading group. Mrs Mata then turned their attention to reading a story.)

T: Vamos a leer un cuento. Vamos a leer para secuencia [sic]. ¿Qué es secuencia? [We're going to read a story. We're going to read for sequence. What is sequence?]

V: Lo que pasó primero, segundo y tercero. [What happened first, second, third?]

T: (She focused the students on the story by calling out the page number.) Página 42, ¿dónde vive Kate? [Page 42, where does Kate live?]
(The students silently read p. 42 while Mrs Mata left the group to check on other students at their seats. When the teacher returned to this group, she posed the same question.)

> T: ¿En dónde vive Kate? [Where does Kate live?]
>
> R: Un apartamento en la ciudad. [An apartment in the city.]
>
> T: ¿Porqué no pudo salir? [Why couldn't she go out?]
> (The children read silently, then answered the question when the teacher called on one of them.)
>
> M: La mamá no quería que andara en peligro en la calle. [Her mother didn't want her to be on the street.]
>
> T: Si. Está bien. Ahora ya tenemos que parar aquí por hoy. Para mañana ustedes tienen que leer hasta la p. 54 en sus libros y contesten las preguntas en la p. 55 en frases completas, más un resumen de una página del cuento. [Yes. That's fine. Now we have to stop for today. For tomorrow, you have to read to p. 54 in your books and answer the questions on p. 55 in complete sentences.]
> (The entire lesson lasted twenty-five minutes.)

The students concentrated on the practice of those skills dictated by the reading text and workbook. During the lessons Mrs Mata called only on the boys to identify words in the vocabulary drill. Her tendency to acknowledge only the boys might be explained by her need to discipline them. She felt more confident that Rita could focus her attention on the lesson while the boys tended to become distracted.

The discussion following the reading of the story centered on specific factual questions related to the text. This search for answers in the text emphasized that the textbook and the teacher were the primary authorities. The information which the children provided about the story was evaluated by the teacher only for its factual accuracy. While the textbook and the teacher are important sources of knowledge, the reading activity did not include any opportunity for students to expand their analytical and interpretive skills. To develop students' higher level thinking, the teachers would have had to utilize the children's cultural experience. This cannot be done by depending on a formulaic set of questions and answers; rather it requires contexts in which recall skills are minimized and more analytical skills are emphasized (Au and Jordan, 1981; Cole and Griffin, 1983; Duran, 1983; Flavell *et al.*, 1981).

Workbook writing exercises were also part of teacher-student interaction. They usually occurred after the group discussions. The workbook problems usually required students to fill in the blanks with facts about the story. A frequent task required students to summarize the story and answer details about the main character. The teacher corrected and graded the students' workbooks each day after school. She reminded them that the last question in the workbook called for a summary of the story about Kate.

In the summary assignment students added their interpretation. Marco's summary illustrated the nature of students' answers to the workbook questions, including the story summaries. This example points to a frequent problem in the students' workbook lessons.

> Kate le decía a su mamá que quería jugar afuera de la casa alta pero era peligro le decía su mama. Pobrecita tenía ganas de jugar. Mi mamá dice que no debemos jugar en la calle y me pongo triste. [Kate told her mother that she wanted to play outside the big house (high rise building), but it was dangerous her mother told her. Poor (girl) she wanted to play. My mother says not to play in the street and I get sad.]

The teacher wrote 'NO' in capital letters. The teacher explained that the students had to learn how to answer the question asked in the textbook and she was not going to accept anything else. The teacher undoubtedly had high standards for her students, and her evaluation reflected the belief that the only correct answer was that which the teacher's manual suggested. The student, on the other hand, appeared to be responding emotionally to the question about the girl's inability to play outside her house. The teacher's reluctance to accept this as an adequate response to the workbook question indicated that there was a difference of interpretation between the student and teacher on what the question asked. The teacher expected students to get their answer exclusively from the textbook, while the children often included their previous experience in addressing the questions.

Advanced Reading Group

The second grade advanced reading group comprised five students (see table 5). Mrs Mata called the advanced group (Vivian, Maria, Rafael, Juana and Nano) to a table in front of the room and drilled them in new vocabulary words for less than three minutes. The daily routine was similar to that for the novice reading groups. Words were flashed to the students, who took turns calling out the correct words. The teacher then questioned the students about the story they read. The following example of student-teacher interaction illustrates how the teacher spent very little time questioning students of this advanced group in a discussion about the story because the students got the main idea quickly; but the teacher failed to expand on the ideas so that students could apply their personal experience.

(The five students in this group gathered around the rectangular table near the chalkboard. The two boys in the group sat next to each other at one end and the three girls sat next to the teacher. Mrs Mata began with a spelling test. The teacher dictated the words and used them in a sentence. The words included 'querer [want]'; 'igual [equal]'; 'idea [idea]'; 'primero [first]'; and 'tierra [land]. While the students wrote their words, they were reminded to write neatly.)

T: Escriban en letra bonita. [Write in nice letters.]

(After the teacher dictated the last word, she left the group to give directions to a student who had arrived late. When Mrs Mata returned to the reading table, the children corrected each other's vocabulary tests. The teacher called randomly on students verbally to provide the correct spelling as they checked the word. Andrea was the only student to get 100 per cent on the spelling test. Mrs Mata announced that because only one person got 100 per cent, the group would have to repeat the test on the following day. The teacher then had the students open their reading books and told them to read the story on 'aviacíon' [aviation] for the purpose of finding the 'idea principal' [principal idea.] The story dealt with scientific principles of aviation equipment, including spaceships, helicopters and planes. Key scientists identified with their inventions and developments in the area of aviation are mentioned in the story.

T: ¿Qué estudian los hombres? [What do the men (in this story) study?]

(The students read silently. After about two minutes, the teacher repeated the question.)

T: ¿Qué estudian los hombres? [What do these men study?]

V: Pájaros. [Birds.]

T: ¿Porqué estudian esto? [Why study this?]

M: Para ir al espacio. [To go to space.]

T: ¿Asíse inventó el avión? [Was this how the plane was invented?]

J: Personas inventan cosas. [People invent things.]

T: Los que estudian. Alguien lea esta parte. [Those who study. Someone read this part.]

(Mrs Mata selects Jose to read orally. Vivian reads next.)

T: ¿Quién fue la persona que hizo volar el avión? [Who was the person who made the plane fly?]

(Teacher asked the question a second time but students did

not respond because they were still looking at their books. She asked a third time and five hands went up and at the same time a student from another group approached the teacher. She turned to him and answered his question. After the boy left, the teacher proceeded to call on Rafael.)

R: Leonardo.

T: Sí, Leonardo da Vinci. ¿Qué inventó? [Yes, Leonardo da Vinci. What did he invent?]

A: Un helicóptero. [A helicopter.]

T: Un helicóptero. ¿Cómo volará? [A helicopter. How does it fly?]

M: Con palitos. [With pointed sticks.]

T: Como una cuerda. ¿Nadie más tiene comentario? ¿Cúal [invención] fue el que tuvo más éxito? Sólo lean la tres línias. [Like a cord wind-up. Does anyone have any more comments? Which (invention) had the most success?]

(A student from another group came to ask the teacher a question and she looked at his paper. When he returned to his seat, she posed the question again.)

M: El globo. [The air balloon.]

T: ¿Porqué fue así arriba? [Because it went up?]

J: Porque tiene aire. [Because it has air.]

(Rafael reads orally from the book to verify Jose's answer.)

T: ¿Qué más ha inventado? [What else has (da Vinci) invented?]

(At this point the teacher left the students to search for the answer in the book while she gave instructions to the teacher assistant. The students debated on what they should be reading. The two boys shared their notion with Maria. Andrea leaned over to ask Vivian a question and Vivian told her to read the rest of the page. Andrea turned her back to the book, put a beaded necklace in her mouth and watched others read. The two boys, Nano and Rafael, began to talk to each other until the teacher returned.)

T: (Asked Maria.) ¿Qué más han inventado? [What else have they invented?]

N: (Nano does not answer.)

V: Jets.

(Without acknowledging Vivian's answer, the teacher announced the next story.)

T: Ahora tienen que leer el siguiente cuento. [Now you have to read the next story.)

(Students want to know if they have read it all.)

T: Sí, y también escriban un cuento de que hicieron durante las vacaciones [de pascuas.]. [Yes, and you also have to write a story about what you did during Easter vacation.]
    (At this point the students are sent to their seats to get their activity workbooks. The workbooks are a compilation of worksheets.)

T: Tienen que hacer la página 21. [You have to do page 21.]
    (On page 21 children had to put words into alphabetical order and write a short summary of the story on aviation inventions. Mrs Mata put an example on the board.)

T: Misa, mesa y masa. ¿Qué letra ven primero? [What letter do you see first?]

J: Masa. La 'a' is first. [Masa. The 'a' is first.]

T: Lean el cuento, escriban sus cuentos y terminen sus libros de actividades. Si no lo terminan, llevenselos a su casa. [Read the story and finish your activity workbook. If you do not complete it, take it home and finish.]
    (Children are dismissed to work at their seats. The lesson lasted twenty-five minutes.)

In this lesson Mrs Mata posed a question then had students search for the answer. She allowed discussion on the subject between teacher and students. She asked if anyone had further comments about the topic before she assigned further reading. Her questions, although mostly fact-based, provoked analytical thinking on the students' part about ways in which the inventions worked. The discussion on inventions, however, dropped off without any conclusion as to the important points that they were to have discovered. If Mrs Mata wanted them to find the 'idea principal', she failed to clarify which one of all the ideas was key. Was it the need to study birds to become informed about space? Was it the significance of da Vinci's inventions? Was it the importance of inventors?

In general the students demonstrated little independence when left alone to search for answers in the book. This illustrates the lack of opportunity that students generally have to think independently not only about the text but about the means by which to find the answer. That is, they may find their answer as long as the teacher explicitly instructs them to read a particular page or paragraph. When called to find the answer themselves, they failed to formulate the relationship between question and answer. The teacher's message to the advanced group was consistent with that to the novice group—that text is entirely a textbook-related event and that what exists in print had little to do with the children's world outside the reading group.

The written products of students in this advanced reading group were evaluated by the teacher on the following day. Aside from the written comments on their papers, no discussion ensued about their writing. The following is an illustration of a writing in which the children had to respond to a question about da Vinci's discoveries.

> (This data sample in Spanish and English has been edited for grammatical errors.)
> Un señor da Vinci descubrió los helicópteros que vuelan con palitos como cuerda. Los pájaros vuelan pero no tienen palitos.
> [The man da Vinci discovered the helicopters that fly with the rotating wing. The birds fly but they don't have rotating wings.]

This student wrote a simple and correct response to the question. He made a comparison between the flying apparatus of the helicopter and birds. Most students wrote something comparable with slight variations in the organization of the facts. The teacher accepted their answers and interpretation of the question and wrote 'OK' on their workbook page. The problem was not that the teacher accepted the students' answers to the question, but rather that she made an arbitrary decision to accept these responses. Mrs Mata did not accept the novice readers' response when they deviated from the expected answers although they demonstrated more forethought and application of the students' experience than did the advanced readers on the subject of aviation discoveries.

Teaching and Second Grade Literacy

The major conclusion from observation of these classroom practices was that, overall, little opportunity existed for higher level thinking skills to be developed in the context of student-teacher interaction. Aside from using Spanish as the language of instruction, the students' knowledge and cultural experience outside the classroom played a minimal role in deriving meaning from text in Mrs Mata's classroom. This is not to say that students did not learn how to read. It means, rather, that the students' learning was minimized by the emphasis placed on factual recall of the text in contrast to the possible benefit of using students' interpretive and analytical abilities (Au and Kawakami, 1984; Cole, 1985; Cole *et al.*, 1971; Diaz *et al.*, 1976). Furthermore, the students learned that status in reading (advanced vs. novice reading groups) was gained by the speed with which they were able to read. This rate was used as the basis for academic evaluation of the students' ability as readers. The context-interaction (Diaz *et al.*, 1976) theory allows us to recognize that these classroom conditions are socially constructed.

Literacy in Mrs Vega's Third Grade

Mrs Vega's third grade class at Marina elementary school had advanced and novice Spanish-speaking reading groups (see Table 6). The advanced reading groups scored at the mean of 76 per cent in the Spanish CTBS, while the mean score for the novice readers was 32 per cent. Students in the novice reading groups read a full year below their grade level. Of particular concern to the teacher were the Spanish-speaking novice readers because they had to learn how to read in Spanish before moving to an all-English reading program. Mrs Vega believed that the seven Spanish-speaking students in her lowest reading group could not comprehend what they read.

On the first day of school students in Mrs Vega's class were assessed on their reading ability and placed in a group along with other students who performed at the same level. She believed that Spanish-speaking students needed to be treated 'very strictly' because that is the best way for them to 'catch up' with the skills that many of the mainstream English-speaking children already possess.

Table 6   *Composition of Third Grade Reading Groups*

	Advanced	Novice
1	Haide Hernandez	Carmen Acosta
2	Betty Mora	Flor Cortina
3	Andrea Ramos	Mona Zamora
4	Lalo Suarez	Jaime Vega
5		Efren Gomez
6		Vicent Vela
7		Rudy Alva
8		Roberto Rosalez

Novice Reading Group

The reading activity for this novice group was conducted in Spanish. Mrs Vega called the students to sit around the table for reading from their textbooks. Written tasks in their workbooks followed at their individual desks. Mrs Vega faced the students to introduce the lesson. Prior to group discussion, the teacher drilled the students in new words in the story or they reviewed their spelling lists.

Following the vocabulary exercises, the teacher asked the students to read and to answer two specific questions which related to the point of the story. The students read individually and silently. The teacher allowed twenty-minutes for the students to read the assigned number of pages. If a story was too long, the teacher assigned only part of it during a period and continued it the following day. Before the teacher even began to ask questions, the students often raised their hands to volunteer an answer. The teacher then posed questions about the reading.

> (During this lesson the eight students in this group (Carmen, Flor, Mona, Jaime, Efren, Vincent, Rudy and Roberto) had been called to the reading table by Mrs Vega. Two of the girls immediately sat on each side of the teacher, who faced the rest of the group. The other children arranged themselves on the remaining chairs. The teacher began by drilling the students on six vocabulary words related to their textbook story ('animales', 'habitaciones', 'mar', 'montāna', 'árbol', 'natural'.) She gave the students the meaning of two of the words 'habitaciones [*habitats*]' and 'natural [*natural*]'. The word drill continued for about twelve minutes during which the teacher went around the table flashing a word card at every student. The next part of the lesson deal with the story which the group had already read the day before. This story, entitled 'Habitaciones Naturales de Animales', detailed three types of animals and their natural habitats and the biological explanations for why the animals chose their respective environments, including climate and food.

> *T:* ¿Cuáles son los diferentes tipos de habitaciones de los animales? ¿Cuál fue la idea principal del cuento? [What are the different types of habitat of these animals? What was the main idea of this story?]
> (No response from students. They look at the teacher but remain quiet.)

> *T:* ¿Cuáles diferentes animales estudiamos ayer? [What animals did we study yesterday?]
> (Students raised their hands and Mrs Vega called on Carmen.)

> *C:* El pez, una lechuza y un lobo. [A fish, an owl and a wolf.]

> *T:* Sí, y ¿dónde viven estos animales? [Yes, and where do these animales live?]

> *M:* Mar, montañas y arboles. [Ocean, mountains and trees.]

> *T:* Está bien y ¿cuáles vivían en esas partes? [That's fine and which ones live in those areas?]
> (All students raised their hands again.)

> *C:* Peces en el mar, los lobos en las montañas y los pájaros en los arboles. [Fish in the sea, the wolves in the mountains and the birds in the trees.]

T: Casi todo está bien, pero no son pájaros, son lechuzas. [Almost all of it is fine, except that they aren't birds, they're owls.]

(All of the students' hands go up simultaneously and they called out, '¡Yo sé! ¡Yo sé!' [I know! I know!] Mrs Vega ignored them and announced a different assignment.

T: Pues, ahora vamos a leer otro cuento. ¿A ver, quién puede leer el primer parráfo? [Well now we're going to read another story. Let's see who wants to read the first paragraph.]

(The story was about a boy with a mischievous dog that the neighbors kept reporting because their gardens were dug up. The teacher called on three different children to read a paragraph in sequence. After they read it, the teacher asked them questions.)

T: ¿Qué problema tiene Roberto? [What's Roberto's problem?]

(None of the students offered an answer.)

T: ¿Qué pasa? Están dormidos todos? Miren, aquí está el segundo párrafo para que lo lean en silencio. [What's happening, Are you all asleep? Look, here is the second paragraph for you to read quietly.]

(The students read silently and Mrs Vega left the group then returned to read more questions from the teacher's manual.)

T: ¿Qué problema tiene Roberto? [What's Roberto's problem?]

E: Su perro es travieso y se enojan los vecinos. [His dog is mischievous and the neighbors get mad.]

V: Escarba los jardines de los vecinos. [It digs up the neighbors' garden.]

T: Muy bien. Ahora sí ya estan listos. Bueno, quiero que acaben de leer este cuento y escriban un resumen sobre cuento anterior de las habitaciones de los animales. [Very good. Now you're ready. Well, I want you to finish reading this story and write a summary on the last story about the animal habitats.]

(At the end of this thirty-minute lesson the students returned to their seats to write the summary.)

Isolated word exercises and fact-related questions characterize this literacy activity. Mrs Vega relied on her teacher's manual to direct her questions to the students. Beyond the manual questions the teacher took no opportunity to expand on various possibilities or to motivate students to ask questions and share their own ideas. The teacher recognized the students' inability to maintain interest in the subject as she attempted to get them to explain Roberto's problem. The real problem may have been that the students did not believe that Roberto had a problem or that his dog's behavior was his problem. This perspective about whose responsibility it was left a great deal of room for interpretation, even if the students later responded that the dog was Roberto's problem. This answer seemed the only possible response to the question which the teacher had clued them to answer by asking the question three times and by having them re-read the paragraph. The limited scope of discussion conveys to the students that the only reason for raising questions is to find a correct answer in the book. This message denies the students' experiential knowledge, as well as the possibility of realizing the integral relationship between the text and the real world.

The written summaries about Roberto's mischievous dog story reflected much the same level of questions as in the teacher-student discussion. The students wrote no more than two sentences which told about Roberto who had a dog that dug up the neighbors' gardens. Most of the students focused on the facts, as Jose's example shows:

El perro [h]acia travesu[r]a[s] y los [v]becinos se enojaban que su jardín estaba esca[r]bado. Roberto no estaba en la casa y los vecinos vinieron por el perro.
(Grammatical mistakes in the Spanish original have been removed in the English translation.)
[The dog was mischievous and the neighbors were angry that he was digging up their gardens. Roberto was not home when the neighbors came for the dog.]

The teacher corrected the grammatical errors in Spanish and returned the papers with an approval indicated by 'OK'. Most of the students' written summaries did not reflect a full account of the story. This may have been due to the limited discussion, as well as the limited time that students had to write. Twenty-five minutes were allocated to the writing activity.

Advanced Reading Group

Mrs Vega had much the same format for the novice group as for the advanced reading group reported here. Advanced group lessons were based on a textbook, the teacher drilled the students in vocabulary at the beginning of the reading lesson then proceeded with discussion of the stories in the book. The following reading lessons exemplified common practice for this third grade advanced reading group.

(Mrs Vega greeted the four students, Haide, Betty, Lalo and

Andrea, after they returned from afternoon recess. The students sat around the large kidney-shaped table near the blackboard.)

T: Ahora vamos a discutir la idea principal del cuento que leyeron ayer, pero primero vamos a repasar estas palabras. Muy muy rápido, rápido, rápido. [Now let's discuss the main idea of the story that we read yesterday, but first let's review these words. Very, very, fast, fast, fast.]

(The words flashed were: 'razón [reason]', 'viaje [trip]', 'ciudad [city]', 'maestra [teacher]' and 'amistades [friends]'. The students jointly called out each of the words as they were flashed by the teacher. After two rounds of flashing the words, the teacher moved on to discuss the main idea of the story. It dealt with a young girl, Lucy, who had moved with her family from Puerto Rico to a big city where they lived with her aunt. Lucy felt very alone because she did not have friends. When Lucy arrived at school the first day, the teacher and the class surprised her with a large potted plant that looked like a palm. They wanted to make her feel at home.)

T: ¿Quién recuerda la idea principal? [Who remembers the main idea?]

E: Yo pienso que la muchacha, Lucy, se sentía triste porque no conocía a nadie. [I think that the girl, Lucy, felt sad because she did not know anyone.]

T: Sí. Es triste no conocer a nadie. ¿Y luego qué pasó? [Yes, it's sad not to know anyone. Then what happened?]

L: La maestra le dió una planta para que se sintiera bien. [The teacher gave her a plant to make her feel good.]

T: Muy bien. ¿Y cómó que penso Lucy de la sorpresa? [Very good. And how did she receive the surprise?]

A: Le gustó porque dijó que tenía amistades. [She liked it because she said that she had friends.]

T: Sí, es lindo tener amistades. ¿Así se sienten ustedes cuando saben que tienen amistades? [Yes, it's nice to have friends. Is that the way you feel when you know you have friends?]
(The students all acknowledged, 'Sí! [Yes!]'.)

T: ¿Dónde está Puerto Rico? [Where is Puerto Rico?]

A: ¿Lejos? [Far?]
(Mrs Vega and all the students laughed.)

T: Sí está lejos, pero ¿dónde está en el mapa? [Yes it's far but where is it on the map?]

T: (She pulled down the map on the blackboard and points out the location of Puerto Rico.) Aquí donde está isla chiquita. Miren aquí estan los Estados Unidos. [Here is the small island. Look here is the United States.]

(Students looked as the teacher pointed. Then she asked a student to show them where Mexico was.)

T: Betty, enséñanos donde está México. [Betty, show us where Mexico is on the map.]

B: (She walking up hesitating.) No sé. Creo que está debajo de los Estados Unidos. (She proceeds to point to Mexico.) [I don't know. I think it's under the United States.]

T: Correcto. [Correct.]

(Everyone applauded. The teacher concluded the thiry–minute lesson by asking students to write a summary of the story on Lucy from Puerto Rico.)

In this illustration the teacher asked the students to tell what the main idea was, but the responses she accepted told more than explaining the significance of the story, which is really what a 'main idea' connotes. As a result of this discussion, it is unclear what the main idea in the story is. Is it that the girl is sad because she doesn't have friends? Is it that she becomes happy when she gets the plant because it means that she has friends? Is it that friends are easy to make? Or is it that moving to a new country may bring fear for children, which is often compensated by friendly surprises? The main point was lost in the discussion which mostly emphasized the facts of the story.

Mrs Vega, however, spent more time attempting to expand the story by asking students to locate not only Puerto Rico on the map but also Mexico, the country of reference for most of the children. The teacher also asked the students to relate their feelings to events in the story: 'Is that the way you feel when you know you have friends?' The question was phrased in such a way that it suggested only a simple 'yes' or 'no' in response. If the students had been asked 'how' they felt in a similar situation, they would have had a better opportunity to express their feelings. Mrs Vega's questions about the story centered on the facts of the story and little discussion ensued about the meaning of the story as it related to the students' sociocultural experience.

The students' written summaries about Lucy's immigration from Puerto Rico reflected mostly a comprehension about the sequence of events. Most of the students wrote about two or three sentences to describe Lucy's situation. The following summary by Andrea is typical.

(The Spanish and English data samples have been edited for grammatical errors.)

Lucy vino de Puerto Rico. Estaba triste que no tenía amigas. La maestra l compró una planta y se sentia mejor. Puerto Rico está lejos y México también. [Lucy came from Puerto Rico. She was sad because she did not have friends. The teacher gave her a plant to make her feel better. Puerto Rico is far and so is Mexico.]

Andrea had the sequence and the facts correct and stated them in a brief manner. She also internalized the fact about the location of Puerto Rico and Mexico. The telling point about Andrea's mention of the location of these countries is that the student heard and incorporated the teacher's extension of the story into her comprehension of the story. Although the point about the location of these countries was a minor way for the teacher to apply the concepts of the story, students found it important enough to include in their writing.

Students' ability to go beyond the facts in the books depends a great deal on higher order thinking questions and the type of discussion encouraged by the teacher. If the students do not participate in literacy activities which require them to think beyond the facts in the book, then it is unlikely that they will learn how to make analytical interpretations and applications in their writing. Such skills are learned in a social context where the teacher relies on students' curiosity for learning and not on the teacher manual.

Reviewing Classroom Literacy

There were no major differences between the reading and written literacy activities in the classroom: the lesson usually focused on simple factual questions posed by the teacher, who used the manual to guide the lessons. A richer interaction between Mrs Vega and the students was reflected in their written summaries.

The data showed that literacy instruction in the second and third grade classrooms had a defined organization. Literacy activities were segmented into rigid isolated areas of vocabulary drill, factual questions and written summaries in which students' interpretations were discouraged. The experiences of the students in the novice and advanced reading groups may be compared.

1 The Spanish-speaking students were divided into advanced and novice reading groups.
2 In both the second and third grades the novice group received substantially more rote memorization vocabulary drilling than the advanced group.

3 The teacher provided a much slower pace for the novice group than for the advanced group. The amount of information covered in the advanced group was greater and on a higher level than for the novice group in the same amount of time. This was due to the teacher's belief that the advanced readers did not need as much drill work because they knew more vocabulary than the novice readers.

4 There was little difference in the type of teacher–student interaction relating to the text. The teachers generally focused on the literal recall of the textbook facts by both advanced and novice groups, with little regard for students' knowledge and experience outside the classroom.

5 Overall teachers evaluated the writing acts differently for the novice and advanced groups. The advanced groups were allowed to interpret the workbook questions in such a way that they incorporated their personal knowledge. The teacher generally approved the responses from these students. On the other hand, students in the novice reading groups were typically held strictly to factual responses based on the text. When the novice readers used their personal experience to respond to the workbook question, this either went unrecognized or was penalized.

6 The teachers' mechanistic use of the curriculum in a prescriptive way was consistent with the school's policy and her professional training. The instructional approach reflected a structural level of reading that emphasized automaticity of vocabulary recognition and factual text comprehension.

7 Students in both classrooms received homework when they did not complete their classroom assignments.

In one respect the teacher appeared to provide more opportunity for the advanced group to express their higher thinking skills than the novice group. In another it appeared that neither the advanced nor the novice group received appropriate structures in which to develop their verbal and cognitive skills. Although these observations of differential treatment in second and third grade literacy activities are not new findings, they describe the student's learning process in deriving meaning from text in the literacy activity. The teacher's beliefs about students' abilities and her teaching competencies are translated into action in her construction of daily literacy activity.

Chapter 5

Home Socialization to Literacy

The home cultural environment is known to play an active role in children's school literacy (Clark, 1984; Goldenberg, 1987; Heath, 1982a, 1982b; Howard, 1974; Schieffelin and Cochran-Smith, 1984; Weisner, Gallimore and Jordan, 1988). It is, therefore, particularly important that we focus on literacy-related activities in the homes of the families in the study. Past research has blamed minority children's school failure on the home culture (Bereiter and Engleman, 1966; Deutsch, 1967), and many educators still believe that minority children are lacking in verbal skills. They feel that parents do not provide adequate exposure to adult talk, which results in a lack of communicative competence. Gordon (1978) explains that these beliefs stem from the assumption that a universal body of information exists about the way that children should be reared and that teachers possess such information and parents should learn it to apply at home. However, variations in childrearing practices among Mexican American families have been documented by researchers (Laosa, 1977, 1978, 1982). Assuming that there is no universal childrearing model (Ogbu, 1981b), how these Mexican families interact with their children in the home in terms of literacy-related tasks is a valid research topic.

One issue that has received less attention than others is the parents' role in the home learning environment of Mexican children. Although much research exists about the direct impact of early home literacy socialization on children's academic performance, much of the material on family literacy activities of Mexican families remains to be examined. Sociocultural knowledge about Mexican family literacy activities tends to relate to the role which parents play in shaping children's cultural knowledge in respect to the family's social networks, socioeconomic conditions and desire to participate in society.

This chapter describes various types of family literacy activities. The issues addressed here pertain to value of literacy (text and non-text) in the day-to-day lives of Spanish-speaking children and their families. How children learn literacy and its purposes is largely a sociocultural process. How children are socialized to literacy in the home influences children's performance in school.

Essential to the discussion of literacy are the household characteristics that are pertinent to socialization into schooling in general and to literacy in particular. Analysis of the data in this chapter was influenced by the emic categories that emerged in Leichter's work. Three general themes are proposed as a way of organizing the catgegories of the study of the socialization to literacy process: *parental aspirations, oral literacy activities, text-interaction activities.* The category of parental aspirations encompasses activities that may be influenced by the parents' educational background and their desire to motivate their children to succeed in school. Factors such as the level of parents' material resources, cultural knowledge about literacy, the family ethnic membership, socioeconomic conditions for social experiences and opportunity to utilize literacy are considered. These characteristics influence family members' interactions with one another in different contexts. The second theme of oral literacy depicts the importance of this form in conveying not only stories but family values, history and affection, as well as language and cognitive skills. The text-interaction theme includes the use of printed text for non-school purposes. The reason for distinguishing non-school from school-related text derives from the observation that most of the printed text activities in the home consist of children's homework. The question of homework subsumes a host of different issues and merits separate treatment (see Chapter 6).

Many activities subsumed under the three themes discussed in this chapter overlap or would fit into more than one theme because they depict numerous aspects of literacy. There three areas, however, encompass home literacy activities and make it feasible to discuss the sociolinguistic, cultural and cognitive characteristics through the 'activity' which unfolds the 'who', 'what', 'where', 'when' and 'why' of the organization (Tharp and Gallimore, 1988; Wertsch, 1985). The assistance provided to children by their parents in text-related interactions provides a context which defines linguistic, cognitive and cultural knowledge transmission necessary to perform these activities.

Parental Aspirations

Spanish is the language commonly used at home by these families. Parents claim that they try to make their children speak Spanish to them and to their siblings. Children in the different families have various levels of Spanish proficiency, but their interaction in the home with siblings takes place in Spanish until they become more proficient in English. This usually occurs by the second or third grade of school.

Adults favor Spanish programs on television from the evening news to 'novelas' (soap operas in Spanish). Many of the younger children also watch television with their parents but as they become more proficient in English, they begin to request their favorite programs in English. Many parents prefer their children to watch TV in Spanish because they expect their children to maintain correct use of Spanish. One parent admitted that he was rather intolerant of poorly spoken Spanish. He instructs his children to watch the news in Spanish and to observe how Spanish is spoken and to practise it. He added, 'Yo creo que si Cervantes escucharia el espanõl que hablan estos niños se voltiaria en su sepulto.' [I think that if Cervantes heard the Spanish that these children spoke, he would turn in his grave.] Parents understand that English is vital to children's participation in society at large, but they also want their children to preserve their native language.

A host of activities engage the children at home after school. In some homes both parents work and arrive home about an hour after the children come home from school. Sometimes these children go to a nearby relative, who may not be employed, or their older high school age siblings may care for them. Some parents, particularly women, work only part-time and are home by the time the children arrive from school. Parents generally insist that children be in their own home or the home of a relative until they arrive home from work. Therefore, children usually do not go to visit friends without parental permission.

Family interactions in the afternoon and evening hours reveal a great deal about the role of parents as educators. Much of the activity revolves around the moment-to-moment business of maintaining a sense of family and accomplishing daily household tasks. What is taught and what is learned during these family events explain a large part of what families consider important about their relationship to one another and to others, as exemplified in the following excerpt.

> Late Tuesday afternoon, Betty came home after swimming in a neighbor's pool after school. Betty's hair was braided. Her mother, Mrs Mora, told her that her hair will get damaged if she left it braided that she should air-dry it instead of braiding it. She instructed her to get a towel and dry it. Betty's 2-year-old sister, Jenny, had candy which she discovered had been eaten while she was out of the room. Jenny began to cry and Rose, an older sister, blamed their older brother. Mrs Mora, however, suspected Rose and told her that it was not right to eat candy that didn't belong to her and that her teeth would fall out. She reminded her of the

fillings in her teeth and the effort that she had to make to not eat candy.

Betty came in the living room with a towel and sat next to her mother who proceeded to comb out the very tangled hair. She began to tell her mother that the water was nice and warm in the pool. She added that she wanted to go to the beach and her mother told her that she'd have to wait till the weekend when she had more time. Betty then asked for permission to go to her friend's house and her mother denied her request because she had already been to a friend's house. Mrs Mora asked Betty if she had finished her homework and she quietly responded 'No'. She then told her mother that Rose colored in her book. Their mother then turned her attention to Rose and told her that it was wrong for her to write in books that did not belong to her.

Mrs Mora established standards for her children's behavior. By not allowing Betty to visit another friend after her swim, Mrs Mora helped her daughter to set a pace for her activities. She advised Betty on the care of her hair by suggesting an alternative to drying it. Simultaneously the mother attempted to correct Rose's actions and instruct her in the difference between right and wrong behavior toward her siblings and material objects like books. Not forgetting her daughter's academic responsibility, she curtailed Betty's social activities because she had not completed her homework. Follow-through was not observed. Mrs Mora's status as a single parent concerned her because she believed that she had to insure that her children learned the proper behavior so as not to embarrass her in public.

Families sometimes use dinner-time not only to share with each other what occurred during the day, but also to reinforce social values as parents comment about the children's activities as well as their table manners. Families do not always eat dinner together because one of the parents may have an evening meeting, the children may eat shortly after arriving from school, or the table may be too small for all of the members to sit together. The Acosta family, for example, had dinner about 5:00 p.m. without the father, who usually arrived home at 7:30 because he had a part-time job over and above his full-time job. Mrs Acosta placed the food on the table and called the four children, Carmen 9, Laura 7, Mary 6, and Lucy 3, to the table. They began their dinner as illustrated here:

Carmen asked for the potatoes and Mrs A reminded her to say, 'por favor'. She did not pass the dish until Carmen said 'please'. The mother then asked each of the girls how their day had been at school. They each answered with a simple 'bien' [good].

Carmen quickly moved the conversation to her sore ankle. Her whining tone conveyed the fact that her ankle hurt and ended by saying with a sigh that all was well. Mrs A reminded her that she had awakened not wanting to attend school and the other children laughed as she admitted to her mother's comment. Carmen, in spite of her ankle, managed to swing and kick her feet under the table throughout the half hour of dinner.

Mary, the younger girl, began to tap a spoon and then asked her mother to pass the salt. Her mother told her to sit up straight and say 'please'. Mrs A realized that she had not served water and apologized. Carmen told her that it was alright. She then apologized for the rice being a bit undercooked. She asked the girls if the salad was OK and Laura explained that she liked the way that the food tasted with chilli on it. Carmen continued the conversation by saying that she wanted to watch a soap opera on TV, which began the following day. Mary requested egg and her mother told her to repeat how one should ask for it correctly. Mary said, 'por favor', and her request was honored. Carmen said that she liked a girl's dress at school and Mrs A acknowledged her with a smile.

Mrs A asked Mary, who is in preschool, if she slept at school and Mary said, 'Sí'. Laura asked if anyone wanted the last meatball before she reached over to help herself to it.

Following a brief exchange about the mild weather, the mother asked Carmen what remained to be completed in her homework. Carmen responded that only math was left and added that the class was practicing for a big test in May, which will consist of twenty-five word problems. Carmen did not know how to say 'word problems' in Spanish. Her mother suggested that it was 'problemas escritas'. Carmen had some difficulty pronouncing it, and her mother, in a rather monotone voice, asked her to repeat it a few times. Carmen proudly announced that she had been moved to the middle group in math and that she was very happy about the change. Her mother commended her and added that just doing one's work and paying attention is all that's required. Carmen added that her group had almost finished the math book to which her mother acknowledged, 'Oh, sí'.

During dinner Mrs Acosta provided her children with an opportunity to share events of importance to them. Although she allowed her children to tell of their interests, she did not share any ideas of her own. The role she played offered authoritative discipline and support to her children. She was interested in having the girls learn how to use polite manners at the table and had them rehearse these behaviors as part of the dinner event. The girls willingly participated. Her other important role was that of an active listener to her daughters. She asked the girls about their day and their activities, and then verbally rewarded them for having accomplished what they wanted as in the case of Carmen. Mrs Acosta's interaction with the girls seemed rather routine and subdued, but the girls were clearly accustomed to having their mother take the time during dinner to ask questions and listen to their interests.

Children develop values about literacy through their interactions with adults in the home. Different levels of activity occurred among family members, in which children developed skills and notions about literacy. Parents consider their children fortunate to have the opportunity to obtain a better education than they had received. Education held the highest priority for these families in a much broader concept than just schooling. Parents referred to the 'buena educación' [good education] in relation to values such as respect, discipline and cooperation. They tended not to teach their children to be aggressive against others for the reason that one parent explained, 'La ignorancia hace a uno creer que la fuerza está en el cuerpo y no en la mente y luego no se ponen a pensar y negociar con la gente.' [Ignorance makes one believe that strength is in the body not in the mind and they do not stop and think and negotiate with others.] Education, nevertheless, is viewed as a vehicle to move children out of poverty.

The desire for children to have a better life than that of the parents accounts for the sacrifices which parents make on behalf of their children. The families in this study shared this goal and they attempted to provide every means possible to support their children's success in schooling. Fundamentally, parents believed that the caring home environment which they create is one of the most important ways in which they can help their children. Many parents share this point of view and believe that such support has to begin at birth.

Moral parameters in a family begin at birth, as most parents concurred. Children need to be molded like clay, to obey because, 'Simplemente tienen que obedecer.' [They simply have to obey.] One father elaborated that the reason children show respect when they get older is that they had been taught how to obey in their early years. Parents agreed that children did not always enjoy being disciplined, and often made faces to show displeasure when they were reprimanded.

Beyond emotional support, many parents guided their children to think about educational activities by purchasing small story books, puzzles, and in some case encyclopedias. On occasion the young children suggested books to their parents to buy when they went shopping because they recognized the cartoon characters on the cover. For older siblings, when purchasing books became less possible, parents encouraged them to go to the library and find books that they liked. Mrs Suarez commented that although she usually relied on the children to bring books home from school once they started reading in first grade, she occasionally took them over to the library.

> Cuando vamos casi siempre es en el verano porque tenemos más tiempo. Durante el año, pues estan en la escuela. Les gusta sacar libros de animalitos, y a mi hijo de aviones y aventuras así. [We usually go during the summer because we have more time. During the year, well, they're in school. They like to check out books about animals and my son likes planes and adventure type books.]

Many of the parents expressed delight that their children wanted to read even when they were not in school and they tried to make time to listen to them read from library books. The children's preschool teacher encouraged parents to engage in reading and conversation with their children and trained many parents to purchase educational materials for their children, take them to the library and read to them at home.

Portillo's parks and beaches provide convenient locations for families to have social gatherings. Many of the men of all ages belong to soccer teams which play at weekends and often involve the whole family as spectators. Family baptisms and first communions are also family social occasions. discussions about these events and preparation for them provide contexts for social interaction and informal education by parents. Many parents who received training with the preschool teacher took advantage of these family events to involve the children in the planning process.

Part of daily learning between parents and children occurred during emotionally packed moments that required immediate parental attention. How the parents dealt with crisis situations often revealed their ability to provide the nurturance and guidance that conveyed caring. Parents made an effort to have children share their feelings and experiences about the emotional events that provoked confrontation between children and parents. This is illustrated by the Dominguez family, when Rita made her first communion.

> (On the day of her first communion, Rita wanted to fix her own hair and her mother insisted on helping her because she wanted Rita's hair to look especially nice. The tension built in the living room and Rita went into the bathroom and locked the door. Her mother followed her and knocked on the door. From outside the door she talked to her:)

M: Mi hija, mira si quieres tu peinarte tu pelo está bien. Yo te dejo que lo hagas tu sola, pero mira escuchame que así no te debes de portar especialmente en este día. Sal mi hija y vamos a hablar nomás. [Dear, look if you want comb your hair, that's fine. I'll let you do it, but listen to me, this is not the way that you should be behaving like this, especially today. Come out and we can talk about it.]

R: Yo quiero una cola. [I want a ponytail.]

M: (She handed Rita a kleenex tissue and wiped her eyes with another one.) Mi hija, hoy es un día muy especial para ti y quiero que te veas muy bonita. ¿Por qué te molesta que yo te peine? [Dear, today is a very special day for you and I want you to look beautiful. Why are you so upset that I want to comb your hair?]

R: No me molesta pero usted siempre quiere hacerme trenzas y yo no quiero. [No, it doesn't bother me, but you always want to make braids and I want a ponytail.]

M: Yo no sabía que no te gustaban las trenzas mi hija. Si quieres te hago una cola. [I didn't know that you didn't like braids. If you want I'll make you a ponytail.]

(Rita continued to cry and her mother wiped her tears and they both went into the bathroom to comb her hair.)

This scenario shows a sensitive conversation between a mother and daughter. It appears that they had not previously communicated about Rita's likes and dislikes about her hair. Mrs Dominguez listened to Rita and considered her desires then tried to reach an agreement that would please both of them so that they could get to the church for Rita's first communion. Through Mrs Dominguez' use of negotiation and authority, Rita confided in her mother about her dislike for braids and her preference for a ponytail. Their ability to arrive at an agreement demonstrated that children and parents in this family use language to resolve prolems. This allowed them to proceed with their special event with understanding.

Although parents most often read to their younger children in the preschool, kindergarten and early grades, they continued to interact with their older children about books even if not actively reading. Many parents felt inadequate about guiding their children in schoolwork once they began to read in English. Some, however, believed that it was necessary to support the older children by motivating them to study.

(Jorge is the junior high school student in this interaction. He is bilingual but prefers to speak in Spanish. He gets mostly 'B' and some 'A' grades in school, but is very bored. He claims to be going to school only because he knows the consequences would be even more painful at home if he were to drop out.)

Son: [Makes an undirected statement.] Ya nomás me faltan tres días de summer school. [I only have three days left of summer school.]

Mother: Aha, pero eso no quiere decir que vas andar de vago. [Yes, but that doesn't mean that you can run around.]

Father: [Laughs] Tienes que trabajar. [You have to work.]

N: ¿Trabajar en qué? Yo trabajo bastante en esa escuela aburrida. [Work in what? I work plenty hard in that boring school.]

M: Pues tienes que estudiar algo que te interese. Ponte a leer y practicar lo que te interesa. [Well you have to study something that interests you. Read and practise something that you like.]

N: Pero no me dejaron entrar a la clase de arte en el centro. [But they didn't let me into the art class at the community center.]

M: Pero tu mismo puedes estudiar y enseñarte si de veras estas interesado en arte. Ve a la biblioteca y saca los libros que te interesen o libros del arte del mundo. ¿Qué crees tu que ser un artista es nomás dibujar? Cuando seas artista, te van a buscar para pedirte tu punto de vista tocante al arte y que les vas a decir si no te has educado. [You have to study and teach yourself if you are really interested in art. Go to the library and get books you're interested in or books about world art. What do you think, that being an artist is just drawing? When you're an artist, they'll look for you to ask for your opinion about art and what are you going to tell them if you haven't educated yourself.

F: Los artistas grandes de Mexico como Orozco y Frida Kahlo sabían no sólo de su arte pero del arte de todo el mundo. Por eso eran famosos. [The major artists in Mexico like Orosco and Frida Kahlo knew not only their own art but that of the whole world. That's why they were famous.]

S: Yo sé pero yo creo que ya estoy programado en la escuela a leer nomás así rápido para contestar las preguntas aburridas que me hacen los maestros. [I know but I think I'm programmed in school just to read quickly in order to answer the boring questions that the teachers ask.]

M: Pero mi hijo si tu mismo te interesas en saber, vas a leer con calma e interés.]But, my dear, if you are interested in learning, you'll be able to read with patience and interest.]

S: Pues a ver. [Well, I'll see.]

(Three weeks later an observation made in the home revealed the following.)

(Jorge went to the library to check out two books, one on Mexican art and the other on Egyptian art.)

Jorge: I went to the library and got these two books. But, I've only started reading the one on Mexican art. It's pretty interesting. It talks about Quetzalcoatl and other Aztec gods and how the Indians worshipped them. They used to sacrifice people to the different gods. I haven't gotten very far 'cause my friends keep coming over and they want me to be with them. So I don't know how long it'll take me to read all those books. But what I really want is to be an artist and I guess this is what I have to know.

Talk in the home plays a major role in the development of familial relationships, ideas and practices which shape children's meaning of their experiences. Many activities in this home provided an opportunity for parents to interact with their children about reading books and other materials, as well about communication with family members in Mexico. These activities became experiences for the children as well as a time to internalize values about the use of books and writing as a way of learning about people and things that they love.

Many parents view themselves as the most important motivators for their children's choice of career and desire for learning and succeeding. One father, Mr Alonzo, stated:

Si tiene un interés para seguir una carrera, pues mejor. El interés que tenemos es de que si ellos tengan la cabeza que les ayude a estudiar. Si Dios quiere que agarren una carrera pues mejor. Siquiera que sepan defendese ellos solos. Porque ahora tanto se ve que ya no sale uno de aqui. Hay tanta familia que ya no quiere estudiar. Uno quisiera lo mejor para sus hijos pero a veces no sale como uno lo piensa. [If she (Vivian) is interested in pursuing a career, well all the better. Our interest is in them and for their mind to assist their learning. If God wants them to have a career, well that's even better because at least they can defend themselves. Today there's so much (bad) that exists out there that one can't leave their home. We want the best for the family, but sometimes it doesn't turn out like we plan.]

Mr Alonzo expressed his desire for his daughters to exercise their full potential so that they could feel secure and protect themselves. He is interested as a parent in supporting his daughters' wishes to study and succeed.

Career planning by children in these families was also a conscious topic of conversation in many homes because teachers stressed the many job possibilities and type of schooling required for different careers. Parents encouraged their children to talk about their ideas and career plans rather casually in these families. Older siblings talked to their parents about their desires once they finished high school. However, the reality is severe for many who had not achieved well and had few alternatives apart from going to junior college or working in the nurseries and fast-food counters. Younger children in the elementary grades talked about their wishes for the future, while parents attempted to interject their own vison.

> Marta sat on the couch giggling and talking with her mother who had just arrived from working at a sewing factory. She told her mother that she knew what she wanted to do when she grew up. Her mother questioned herand Marta replied that maybe she didn't know exactly the job. She sat and thought for a couple of minutes. Martha said that she liked flowers and so a nursery would be fine as a place of employment. Her mother laughed and said, 'Nursery?' Marta's mother told her that the most important thing was to think of a career, something useful so that Marta would not have to work as hard as she has had to all her life. Marta then said that she would be a teacher. Her mother approved of her choice. She assured Marta that teachers also work hard but she would not have to work exhaustively from sunrise to sunset. Marta continued to fantasize about being a doctor so that she could work in a clinic so that she could help children and the elderly. Quickly she added that perhaps she would like to be policewoman like in the television series, 'Chips'. This sparked Marta's memory about the previous day's 'Chips', and she began to relate the details of the episode. Her mother just sat and listened to her.

Families share a great many activities in the home that contribute to the children's orientation to the world and their place in it. Parents utilize day-to-day events to socialize their children into values about the importance of education, to communicate with others members of the family, to support and shape career interests and in general to demonstrate family cohesion.

Oral Literacy Activities

(In this scene the mother showed family pictures to three of her children, Juan, Elena and Bobby, aged 12, 10 and 7 respectively.)

Mother: Miren quienes son estos. ¿Se acuerdan quienes son estos niños? (He pointed to the pictures in the family album.) [Look, who are they? Do you remember who these kids are?]

Elena: Mis primos. [My cousins.]

Mother: Sí. [Yes.]

Juan: ¿Dónde viven? [Where do they live?]

M: En Michoacán. ¿Sabes donde está? [In Michoacan. Do you know where that is?]

All: En México. [In Mexico.]

E: ¿Por qué viven alla? [Why do they live there?]

M: Porque sus papás tienen un rancho allá. [Because their parents have a ranch over there.]

M: ¿Se acuerdan cuando visitamos allá hace dos años? [Do you remember when we visited there two years ago?]

B: No, yo no. [No, I don't.]

M: Porque tu estabas muy chiquito, eras un bebé. [That's because you were very small, you were just a baby.]

M: ¿Y ella quién es? [And who is this?] (Points to the picture of an older lady.)

All: 'Buelita. [Grandma.]

M: ¿Les gustaría visitarla en su rancho otra vez? [Would you like to visit her in her ranch again?

E: A mí sí. Me gustan los animales. [I would. I like the animals.]

M: ¿Qué más se acuerdan del rancho? [What else do you remember about the ranch?

All Caballos y gallinas y muchas cosas. [Horses and chickens and lots of things.]

M: Les gustaría vivir allá? [Would you like to live there?]

J: No, es muy aburrido porque no tienen TV ni cines. [No it's really boring because they don't have TV or theaters.]

M: Es cierto que no tienen esas cosas pero es que ustedes ya se acostumbraron a vivir aquí (en los Estados Unidos).

[That's true but it's because you've become accustomed to living here (in the United States).]

This event provided an opportunity for the mother to remind the children of their family and visits to Mexico. The children expressed interest in staying in the United States and the mother surmised it was because they had become accustomed to the conveniences. The daughter, however, wanted to visit the cousins and the ranch in Mexico.

Parents did not always read to their children as a way of sharing time and ideas with them. Oral folklore about popular characters was also a popular pastime. Oral lore practices did not necessarily indicate illiteracy on the part of the parents, rather they served as a frequent form of recreation for families, even those who read storybooks to their children. Both mothers and fathers used this form of communication with their children to promote closeness through humor. On Sunday afternoons, or early evenings after dinner when the homework was completed, children could sometimes be heard soliciting their parents to tell them their favorite story, 'Papa, dinos un cuento de esos chistosos.' [Dad, tell us one of those funny stories.] The stories tend to become a family event because everyone likes to take part in embellishing the story.

In the following Mr Alva showed that communication with his children can be a truly amusing pastime in which children's cognitive skills are challenged.

(After the family returned from a picnic on a Sunday evening, Rudy ran to his father and told him to tell a story. The mother was in the kitchen cleaning up and kept one ear on the story while the father proceeded to regale Rudy and his sister, Sonia, with a version of Little Red Riding Hood.)

Father: Ok, este es el cuento de Caperucita Roja que quería comerse un lobo. [OK, this is a story about Little Red Riding Hood who wanted to eat a wolf.]

Mother: ¿Cómo que Caperucita se iba comer a un lobo? Mi hijo alegale, dile que no esta corecto. [How can Red Riding Hood try to eat the wolf? Son, challenge him, tell him it's wrong.]

Sonia: ¿Cómo se llamaba el lobo? [What was the wolf's name?]

F: (He laughs.) Sí había un lobo que se llamaba Fidencio y luego había tres cochinitos que se querían comer al lobo. [Yes, there was a wolf named Fidencio and then there were three pigs that wanted to eat the wolf.]

Rudy: ¿Cómo se llamaban los cochinitos? [What were the pigs' names?]

F: Puerco, Cochino y Marrano. Esos marranitos querían comerse al lobo y entre los tres planeaban como le iban a mochar una pata al lobo porque no querían desperdiciar la carne. Luego la iban a cocinar y ya estaban hambrientos pensando como iban a capturar al lobo. [Pig, Porky and Fatso. Those little pigs wanted to eat that wolf and they plotted how they would cut off one of his legs cause they didn't want to waste food. Then they would cook the leg and they were getting real hungry just thinking about capturing a wolf.]

S: No entiendo por que nomás una pata le iban a mochar al lobo. [I don't understand why they were only going to chop off one of the wolf's legs.]

F: Pues, es que no tenían 'freezer' y la carne se hecha a perder si no la guardan bien. [Well they didn't have a freezer and the meat spoils if you don't store it properly.]

M: Pregúntenle que cómo alcanzaron al lobo. [Ask him how they caught the wolf.]

F: Los marranitos lo esperaron y lo atacaron y le mocharon una pata. El pobre lobo luego se fue cojeando y no sabía que hacer ni como caminar. [The pigs waited for him then they jumped him and they cut off his leg. The poor wolf didn't know how he would walk.]

S: Pero papi, como puede ser posible eso porque el lobo es muy furioso por que no se peleó con los marranitos? [But, dad, how is that possible cause isn't the wolf an angry animal and why didn't he fight the pigs?]

F: Pues es que entre los tres marranitos le ganaron con la fuerza, y mejor se fue a ponerse una pata de palo para poder caminar. [Well between the three pigs they won with force and the wolf thought it was better to go and make himself a wooden leg to be able to walk.]

S: ¿Una pata de palo? ¿Cómo se puso él la pata? [A wooden leg? How did he put on his wooden leg?]

F: Sí, él se la clavó, ¿a ver dónde quedamos? Luego el lobo dicidio que se iba comer a los cochinos y al lobo se le salía la baba de pensar en las patas del cochino. [Yes, he hammered it on, now let's see where were we? Then the wolf decided that he was going to eat the pigs and the wolf foamed at the mouth just thinking about the pigs' legs.]

S: ¿Pues papá cúal se iba a comer primero? Primero dijiste

Puerco y luego Cochino. [Well which one is he going
to eat? First you said the Pig then Porky.]

F: Pues uno por uno iban a cortarles las patas y a comerselas
pero quería también a transplantarles las patas. [Well he
was going to eat one at a time but he also wanted to
use two of the legs to transplant them for the ones he
had lost.]

S: ¿Papá, pero cómo sí las patas del marrano son tan chiquitas
y las del lobo son tan largas? [Dad, but how is it possible
if the pigs' legs are so short and the wolf's are longer?]

F: Sí pues, eran cuatro marranos y podía escoger las patas
que le midieran más bien pero aunque eran más cortas,
pero el lobo iba a usar pantyhose para que no se vieran
tan mal. [Yes, there were four pigs and he had lots of
legs from which to choose the legs that fit him and even
if they were shorter but the wolf was going to use
pantyhose so that they wouldn't look bad.]

Sonia demanded clarification from her father as to which of the pigs the
wolf actually ate. She also challenged his sense of logic about the leg size
involved in the transplant from the pig to the wolf. The questions raised
by the children show the children's search for meaning in the story. The
father further embellished the story, using contemporary objects like the
pantyhose to hold the children's attention. Sonia giggled about her father's
responses.

Sonia: (She giggled and laughed.) No dad you made one up.
(Statement was made in English.)

Father: No son tres—Marrano, Puerco, Cochino. [No there
were three—Pig, Porky and Fatso.]

S: Sí, pero tu dijiste cuatro and there are only three
(codeswitched).

F: Sí, Caperucita y el lobo prepararon el caso con manteca
para meter a los cochinos. [Yes, Little Red Riding Hood
and the wolf prepared the pot with lard to put the three
little pigs in there.]

S: ¿Pero cómo prepararon el caso si andaban en el bosque
sin nada? [But how did they prepare the pot if they were
in the woods without anything?]

F: Pues, Caperucita fue a llevarle el lonche a su abuela y
luego trajo el caso y al fin pescaron al marrano y le
cortaron las patas para que sintiera lo mismo que sintió
el lobo. [Well, Little Red Riding Hood went to take

S: ¿Y que iba hacer con la carne? [And what did they do with the meat?]

F: Pues, tenían que comersela muy pronto porque no tenían 'freezer'. [Well, they had to eat it fast because they didn't have a freezer.]

R: ¿Y no le apestaban las patas? [And didn't his hoofs smell?]

F: Sí, pero las hirvieron bien y así salieron muy sabrosas y hasta invitaron a Pinocho. [Yes, but they boiled them well and they turned out delicious and they even invited Pinocchio.]

S: ¿Pinocho? Pero papa, Pinocho vive muy lejos. [Pinocchio? But dad, Pinocchio lives far away.]

F: Sí, pero vino a acompañarlos. [Yes, but he came to accompany them.]

S: ¿Y los otros marranos? [What about the other pigs?]

F: También uno por uno los alcanzaron y les mocharon las patas luego ellos tuvieron que andar con muletas. [They too were caught and their legs were cut off so they had to walk around on crutches.]

The Alva family revelled in the folkstory event that children requested. Mr Alva used several popular characters to weave together his story with the assistance of the family members. At the beginning Mrs Alva provoked the children to challenge the father's story, and they were cued to ask questions to move the story along. This example demonstrates the cognitive flexibility of parents to convey meaning and enhance children's cognitive skills. By relating the content of what their father is telling them to the traditonal story, the children were forced to negotiate a story. Rudy listened and had only two clarifying questions, while Sonia followed the story's logic and forced her father to respond to her questions to her satisfaction. Although most of the story was told in Spanish, Sonia made two comments to her father in English. while it is clear that he comprehended her statements, he continued his story in Spanish.

Text–Interaction Activities

The practice of reading to children, for most of these families, has been acquired through their contact with the bilingual preschool teacher who treated the parents as co-teachers. Parents made purchases at a local bookstore that has teacher supplies. Most of the parents who read to children usually did so after dinner. While parents watched television, children meandered in and out of the living room and often requested the parent to read them a favorite story. Mothers read to the younger children more than fathers. It was rare to see a parent reading to a child who was more than 8 years old, although occasionally an older brother or sister sat nearby and listened inconspicuously while the parent read to younger children. In most cases younger children under 8 years of age engaged their parents to read to them as a form of entertainment. Who, what and where the parents read to children mattered less than how parents shared stories with their children. The following illustrates how Mrs Hernandez read to Raul, her 5-year-old son.

(This activity involved reading a small Walt Disney book one evening after dinner. The mother was watching TV and the child brought the *Caperuciti Roja* storybook to her to read to him. She held the book and began to read.)

Mother: Este cuento es de Caperucita Roja y el lobo. Tu ya te lo sabes de memoria. [This is the story of Little Red Riding Hood and the wolf. You already know it by heart.]

Son: No, no, no me lo sé. Quiero que me lo leas. Me gusta el lobo. [No, no, no, I don't know it. I want you to read it to me. I like the wolf.]

M: (The mother turned the page and began to read.) Había una vez una niña que se llamaba Caperucita Roja. Ella le llevaba comida a su abuelita. Iba muy feliz por el campo hasta que se encontró con un lobo. UUUUU iiii uuuu el cucuy (sic). [Once there was a little girl named Little Red Riding Hood. She was taking dinner to her grandmother. She was walking through the woods until she ran into a wolf. OOOO eeee OOOO the boogie man.]

(The mother continued to hold the book and turn the pages. She stopped reading the text and improvised the narrative by looking at the illustrations.)

M: Oh y ese lobo, estaba bien hambriento. Y seguía a Caperucita. Miralo ahi íba atrás de ella. [Oh, see the wolf, he was very hungry. He followed Red Riding Hood. Look there he goes behind her.]

Raul: Quería comersela. [He wanted to eat her.]

M: No, no quería comersela, quería los tacos que le llevaba a la abuelita. [No, no, he didn't want to eat her, he wanted the tacos that she was taking to her grandmother.]

M: ¿Qué crees que hizo Caperucita? [What do you think Red Riding Hood did?]

R: Mató al lobo. [She killed the wolf.]

M: Pero antes. (She called the son's attention to the picture.) Mira, comenzó a correr y correr. [But before. Look at how she ran and ran.]

R: Porque no quería que el lobo la alcanzara. [Because she did not want the wolf to catch her.]

M: Sí, pero luego ella le hizo un truco y, ¿qué pasó? [Yes, but then she tricked him, and what happened?]

R: Yo sé. Ella llamó a la policiá. [I know. She called the police.]

M: Que inteligente mi hijito. Ahora ya sabes que hacer tu si te sigue un lobo. ¿Verdad? [How intelligent, my dear. Now you know what to do when a wolf chases you. Right?]

(The child took the book and ran into his room and the mother went into the kitchen to wash the dinner dishes.)

Mrs Hernandez showed a concern to relate the text to the child's present situation, such as the need for Raul to be alert in his surroundings. The mother also used this opportunity to dramatize the story to make it more interesting. She contemporized the plot by using culturally familiar food. Most importantly, Mrs Hernandez captured Raul's attention and held it by posing questions to him about the story, using his linguistic and cognitive skills. Raul offered his comments and predictions about characters in the story.

Raul, too young to read indpendently, revelled in sharing the story his mother read to him. Other children older than Raul read independently. Most parent-child interaction about text took place in Spanish because of the parents' limited proficiency in English. On rare occasions, however, the children read to their parents in English and, depending on the parents' facility with English, they directly assisted in the reading process. In the following illustration, a third grader, Andrea Ramos, read the storybook *Heidi* to her father.

Andrea: On top of a mountain of the Swiss Alps, Heidi lived with her grandfather. Their home was a hut overlooking the village.

Father:	Valley.
A:	valley and be
F:	behind
A:	behind stood old
F:	three old
A:	three old fir tree — tree
F:	trees.
A:	trees. Heidi lo
F:	loved
A:	loved to hear
F:	the wind
A:	rushing and rolling in the long thick branches. Heidi had a happy life. In the summer she went up the mountain with Pe — : Peter
A:	Peter. She knew the names of the
F & A:	flowers and she was
A:	fir — : friends
A:	friends with all the goats. In the winter time she stayed inside with grandfather to help him ham
F:	hammer
A:	hammer together chairs and tables. Sometimes Peter would stir-r--
F:	struggle up the snowy
A:	struggle up the snowy paths to call for Heidi and took her down to visit his mother and grandmother.

Here Mr Mora assisted Andrea to read the story. Although the father seemed to correct many words for Andrea, sometimes he did not wait for her to make an error, he actually read along with her as in the line 'flowers and she was'. It was as though he anticipated some of her areas of struggle. Part of this interaction that may not be obvious from the transcript is that this father was particularly proud of knowing English and of his ability to use it to help his children. In this case he did not allow Andrea to struggle with the text before assisting her. He had been taking English as a Second-Language classes and had been progressing confidently. The activity continued in much the same way.

F and A:	Many weeks went by and Heidi grew more and more sick.
A:	The same doctor that came to see Clara saw that she had grown sick and pale with home sickness. He said, 'You must send her home at once.'
F:	Start up here on top. (He pointed to the top of the page.)

A: (She nodded yes and continued). They packed her bags and they took her up to the mountain she loved so much.

This reading event represented the active role that parents play in helping their children read a story with minimal interpretation offered at the time of reading. Their limited English-speaking ability need not interfere with children and parents reading English. The father plays a role comparable to that of the teacher who tells the child the word in order to promote fluency. In this case Andrea and her father seemed to be motivated by the need to share in their accomplishment of completing the story.

Shaping a child's ability to comprehend ideas was revealed through numerous home activities. How children learn to think about themselves, as well as about their social and physical environment, often involved the engagement of parents and children in relation to written text. Reading and writing at home sometimes had a non-academic or pragmatic goal. Children read letters from their relatives in Mexico and often wrote letters in return. Parents indicated that some children required more encouragement than others to write to relatives in Mexico. The letter writing session sometimes occurred during the homework period, but at other times they wrote brief notes to add to their parents' letters. Correspondence between the children in Portillo and their cousins, aunts and grandparents usually recounted the special events and expressed the children's esteem for their family members. The adult family members include more detail in their letters. Often relatives in Mexico had visited Portillo and become close to the children so that after family members returned to Mexico the children found it easy to continue their relationship. In the case of Sara, whose letter appears below, she learned English because she studied it while visiting Portillo. Writing to nieces and nephews provided an opportunity to practise English. Each of the samples shown here was written at different times by members of the same family in Mexico and Portillo. Letter 1 wa written to two children in the Suarez family. The oldest child, Miguel, is in junior high school and knows English quite well so that Sara usually writes to him in English. The letters written in Spanish presented in their original form with edited and translated English versions.

Letter 1

Guadildjara Zal.

Hi Carlos:
Como estas mijo espero que muy bien. Como te va en la escuela? A que

grado vas a entrar? Tingo muchas ganas de verlos a todos te portas bien con tus papas y se culida mucho

> Te Quiere
> Tu tia
> Sara]

[Hi Migual Jr.
How are you? They showed me a picture of you and you're one handsome fellow. So are you going into High School? I'm very proud of all of you

> See you soon
> Love you
> Sara

P.S. I want a picture of you. O.K.

Letter 2

Estimada Tia, Sara
    Como esta mi papa y los demas. Como va la cosa para que no esten solos aya. Como estan mis tios y tias. Por favor de saludarme a mi tia ramona y mi papa polo.

> Lalo

[Dear Aunt Sara,
How is my papa and the rest. How is everything. I want everyone to come [over here] so that you won't be all alone over there. How are my aunts and uncles. Please say hello to aunt Ramona for and my daddy.

> Lalo]

    Veronica also knows English well but prefers to practise her Spanish when letters from Aunt Sara arrive. Veronica also received mail from her cousin, Maribel, who is interested in having her visit for her 'quincienera' (fifteenth birthday).

Letter 3

Mayo 25 de 1988
Querida vero disculpa que me atrase en escribirte:
    Vero no Estoy en la escuela como tù me mandas decir Pero e estado ocupada de un tado para otro tù sabés no. mira Lupe y yo pensabamos escribirte igual bueno vero despues de saludarte paso alo Siguiente.
    Vero te espero para el dia de mis 15 aõs el 20 de Agosto de 1988 no te puedo decir donde va hacer la celebracion yo despúes te digo espero y vengas por favor vero si bienen me haras feliz ese dia con tu presencia bueno es todo lo que te digo contestame pronto si vas a benir si no por

favor que caiga tù carta ese dia de mi compleaños pero espero y mejor estes ahi

Adios VERO
MARIBEL DIAZ

Dear Vero forgive me for the delay in writing you. Very, I'm not in school like you tell me but I've been busy in other ways as you can understand. Lupe and I have been thinking about writing you but now let's go on to something else.

Vero, I await you for my fifteenth birthday the 20 August 1988. I can't tell you where the celebration will be. I'll tell you later. I await you and if you come, you'll make me very happy that day with your presence. Well that's all that I have to say. Please write soon if you're going to come. If you can't come, I hope that at least your letter to me will arrive on my birthday, but I hope to see you there.

Good bye Vero
Maribel Diaz

Leticia, a first grader, also likes to stay in touch with her aunts in Mexico. In this letter Leticia wanted to know about her father who had gone to Mexico to visit his ailing mother. Leti wrote the letter in a stressful situation. Her mother, who was running errands on a Saturday in September, had promised to drop off the letter at the mailbox on her way to the market if she finished it on time, and Leti was most anxious about writing to her Aunt Romano because of her father's visit to his family.

Letter Sample 4

9188 3

éstimada tia Ramona como esta mi Papá como estas tia yo te estime mocho y com es ta mi tio y lo es timo mu chio y como esta la casa y ojata que todo se arregte y saludós a mis tios y tia los guiero a te dos familia estodos que todo este viehy todo en el mundo que qiero mas que ustedes y los qiero todos y estero que todo salga vien y los qiero mas que nada y et estero que todo es te vien y estodo ti y astolvegos

be Let

tio Raul   tia Sara   tio chuy papa

[Dear Aunt Romana,
How is my dad. How are you aunt.. I love you very much and how is
my uncle. I love him too. How is the house. I hope everything will turn
out fine. Say hello to my uncles and tell them that I love everyone. The
thing I want most is for everyone to be fine and I hope that everything
turns out fine. I love you more than anything.

Kisses, Leti

The letters from Aunt Sara and Maribel show a lot of love and
appreciation for the children. It is also apparent that the text in Spanish
and English from the Mexican relatives ignores some of the conventions
of grammar and punctuation, while the letter written by Lalo, who is
a fourth grader, is more observant of academic rules. A possible
explanation is that Lalo wrote his letter following his homework session;
his mother, Mrs Suarez, monitors the children's writing and work
completion during their homework. The exception in these samples was
Leticia's letter which was written in a hurry for her mother to get it in
the mail box on her way to the market. In all her rush, however, Leti
found time to draw pictures of her Uncle Raul, Aunt Sara, Uncle Chuy
and her father at the end of the letter.

Summary

Home literacy activities provide a framework for observing parents as
educators in their natural social milieu. Literacy existed in these homes
in forms ranging from emotional support for the children to pursue
schooling to storybook reading by parents. Embedded in activities and
interactions in their daily routine, they demonstrate how children and
parents jointly build meaning. Exchanges about family events, the
importance of schooling and oral folklore provide occasions for parents
to engage with children through the use of language. Children's verbal
and non-verbal communication gives rise to parents' comments
reinforcing values important to the family. More text-related activities,
including reading to children from storybooks, writing to relatives in
Mexico and reading school bulletins force parents to use their literacy
skills in Spanish and English and provide opportunities for children to
translate English material for their parents. Some parents read more to
their children than others, which suggests that those families had learned
through training about the merits of reading to their children. This implies
an effective relationship between the school and the home learning
environment.
Literacy in these homes occurred in multiple discourses through

which adults and children generated meaning in their daily social contexts. Freire and Macedo (1987:154) contend that, 'without understanding the meaning from their immediate social reality, it is most difficult to comprehend their relations with the wider society.' These families show the ability to relate to each other around sociocultural activities, sociolinguistic discourse and written text. It is this meaning that children take to school and it must be considered in the school curriculum.

Non-school-related home literacy activities were diverse and provided an opportunity for learning and levity in the family. However, once the children began reading in structured reading groups in school, homework formed the bulk of learning activity at home.

Chapter 6

Parents' Reponse to Homework Literacy Activities

The Portillo families provided their children with a variety of home learning contexts that appeared to be non–school-related. However, once children were placed in reading groups in the classroom, the majority of home literacy activities became devoted to homework. Classroom literacy followed children into the home. Examination of homework activities created another opportunity to understand the parents' role in their children's schooling and how parents deal with children's classroom literacy lessons. The research discussed here indicates a need to study literacy in the home as a way of understanding the cultural knowledge children bring to school, as well as the knowledge about schools that children bring home. By learning how parents interact with their children in home literacy tasks, we attain a perspective that can inform not only classroom instruction but also parent education efforts to empower families who in turn empower their children (Cummins, 1986).

The family ecocultural niche defines the home setting in which literacy activities are organized. This concept, identified by Super and Harkness (1980) and discussed by Weisner, Gallimore and Jordan (1988), refers to the sociocultural environment surrounding the family, including socioeconomic conditions, political, religious, social and educational networks, as well as the interactions of family members. Personnel, cultural patterns, activities, goals and motives are the elements of activity settings in which teaching and learning occur in the home and which Tharp, Jordan and O'Donnel (1980) are convinced elicit child behaviors with which educators must be concerned.

Parents in the twenty families differed in their schooling experience. While two parents had graduated from the equivalent of high school in Mexico, the median level of formal education was fourth grade (see Table 7). Most of the adults had attended evening English as a Second Language

Table 7   Family Characteristics of Twenty Second and Third Grade Children in Advanced and Novice Reading Groups

Characteristic	Student reading level	
	Advanced (9)	Novice (11)
	(percentages)	
Yearly household income below $13,000	100	100
Six members or less per household	88	82
More than six members per household	11	18
Longer than five years resident in Portillo	44	72
Spanish most frequent home language	100	100
Single parent family	0	11
Four years or less formal education in Mexico	77	72
One parent completed high school in Mexico	22	0.09
Both parents employed full-time	88	82
One parent employed full-time and one part-time	11	18
Laborer or service occupation of adults in household	100	100
One or more children attended bilingual preschool in Portillo	66	27

classes in the community college. They found that learning English was difficult because most of their employment settings at nurseries, on assembly lines and in restaurants required little use of English except for minimal interchanges related to the job. In spite of this lack of opportunity to use English on a day-to-day basis, most parents believed that learning the language was necessary to enable them to help their children in school-related tasks.

A wide range of school achievement existed among siblings within families, similar to that noted by Barnes (1984). Although parents with a higher level of formal education in Mexico often had children who were high achievers in literacy and other subjects, some high achieving children came from homes where the parents had minimal formal education. Parents with minimal Spanish and English literacy expressed feelings of constraint in their ability to do literacy activities with their children, especially school-related tasks. Although they valued schooling for their children, many had only vague notions concerning ways to help them to learn. Parents consistently encouraged their children to behave well in school and learn to read in order to succeed in school and thereby enhance their employability.

All the parents in this study expressed a great desire to have their children succeed in school. Many parents believed that it was increasingly harder to help their children with academic tasks as the students moved into English reading and an all-English curriculum. It was particularly difficult when the children entered junior high and high school because of the complexity of the curriculum. Nevertheless, some parents struggled to prepare their children in numerous ways by providing them with emotional support and encouragement to stay in school.

Table 8 represents the use of time, availability of space and types of parent-child home interaction. All parents made an effort to provide children with a supportive learning environment. Although these parents shared a similar socioeconomic and immigrant status, they interacted somewhat differently with their children. Parents of advanced readers allowed their children more freedom to do their homework. Independence was discussed by parents as a behavior that they encouraged from early on because they wanted children to take responsibility for their work. Parents of novice readers who were less independent explained their insistence on their teaching children discipline to do their homework because the teacher reports usually indicated that they needed more assistance in their homework. Many children performed on at least an average level in school in spite of their parents' inability to assist them directly with their homework. In spite of variations in parental assistance at home, parents of advanced and novice reading students shared a great deal of confusion about what the school expected academically, and they felt equally frustrated about ways to help their children meet academic goals.

Table 8   Practices in Home Literacy Interactions

Practices	Student reading level Advanced (9) (percentages)	Novice (11)
Parents read books (other than homework) with children	77	36
Designated space for homework available	77	45
Parents designated time for doing homework	33	72
Average time spent on homework less than thirty minutes	44	18
Average time spent on homework more than one hour	55	82
Parent typically reminded child to do homework	22	63
Child usually requested assistance from parent during homework	33	63
Parent typically assisted directly during homework	44	54
Parent usually gave child the answer	11	63
Parent usually only checked homework on completion	77	36

Homework Literacy Interaction of Advanced Readers

Strong emotional support for achievement characterized the relationship between parents and children in the advanced group. Of nine students in this group six had attended the district's bilingual preschool, which had an effective parent training component. The bilingual bicultural preschool teacher, a resident of the community, knew the families' home situation. she met monthly with the parents as a class and taught them how to read to their children, to engage them in conversation, and to create learning activities in the home. Two of four advanced readers had not attended preschool, but the parents had learned from the children's teachers that reading with children helped to motivate learning. In the other two families the parents did not read with their children very much in the earlier years. Those parents who did read with them continued the practice more frequently with their children when they were in preschool, kindergarten and at the beginning of first grade. Usually, small popular animal storybooks purchased at major discount stores provided the reading material. As children advanced in school, parents discontinued leisure reading and homework constituted much of the literacy activity in the home. Although the bilingual preschool was a pivot in building awareness among these parents of home–school relationships, systematic parent education efforts were for Spanish-speaking parents limited after the preschool level.

Reading workbook and ditto pages comprised the homework assignments for most students. Most assignments were in Spanish, but some were in English. Parents generally believed that their children were responsible for deciding when to do their homework because they felt that the children understood best their own academic responsibilities. Children usually arrived home and played with their siblings or watched television. They had no fixed time to do their homework. Many of the children in this group did their homework just before dinner while others waited until after dinner.

Parents reported that their children were generally autonomous in completing their homework tasks and requested little assistance (see Table 8). Parents helped by supervising their children. For example, Ester Hernandez's parents claimed that they did not have to help because she usually wanted to do the homework by herself, except when she could not understand the instructions. Her mother explained, 'Yo la dejo que trate de hacer su trabajo, pero aseguro que lo complete antes de que se acueste.' [I let her try and do her work by herself, but I make sure that she completes it before she goes to bed.] Mrs Hernandez's involvement with her children's homework kept her informed of their progress in school. She gave all three children the same attention. Her oldest son had begun to work strictly in English, but she monitored the progress of his homework and had him discuss the completed assignment with her.

Occasionally a child solicited parental help for a problem in English.

Parents would then try to read it in English and translate it into Spanish so they could explain it to the child. A few of the advanced readers received reading exercises in English for homework because the teacher wanted to accelerate their transition into English reading. Although parents in these cases did not usually help to solve homework problems, they held the children responsible by asking to check completed work. The students reported to their parents after finishing their tasks, and the parent listened to the child describe the tasks that had been completed.

Although students in this advanced group usually worked without much direct assistance from their parents, the parents sometimes had to help. The example below illustrates the assistance that, Lalo, a third grade advanced reader, required of one of his parents. They sat at the kitchen table before dinner with Lalo's three siblings and both parents assisting the two children who had homework in Spanish. The two older siblings had homework in English and they worked together. Lalo's assignment required more parental attention than usual on this particular night, as this example illustrates:

> (The parent had to time the vocabularly list. Lalo had to read ten words in one minute. His mother had the clock in front of her and watched the second hand as Lalo read the words. His first two attempts went over the one-minute limit. His mother encouraged him to do it faster.)
>
> M: Ya mero. Mira si puedes pronunciarlas primero así sin el reloj, luego ya tienes practica y no tienes que tropezarte con la pronunciación cuando te estoy marcando el tiempo. [Almost. Look if you pronounce them first and then practice it, you won't trip over the pronunciation when I'm timing you.]
>
> L: OK.
>
> (The mother timed Lalo three more times, and twice he was able to read the words within the minute required. After that exercise the mother had to listen to Lalo read a story from a small reader sent home by the teacher. She listened to him read *El Castillo y El Rey* and occasionally corrected his mispronunciation. He also requested her to assist him about four times during his reading of the story. The vocabulary list and the story took one and a half hours. Following the task, the family ate dinner.)

Although this case exemplifies a successful attempt at completing the task, most parents felt frustrated and confused in helping their children with homework. For tasks that required reading, the parent had to know how to read because they had to know whether the child was reading the correct words. Parents believed that homework was a constant source of anxiety because it was not always as simple as listening to the children read or timing vocabulary exercises. The major problem seemed to be that they never quite knew what the teachers expected or whether students were penalized or rewarded for the work which they spent so much time doing almost every night.

These feelings of frustration became the reason for parental contact with schools to clarify the school's expectations and the child's progress. Although school reports usually praised children in this group for being good students, some parents wrote notes to the teacher or dropped by the school to talk with the teacher whenever possible. They raised concerns about the tasks that the students received which prevented them from helping their children. They often asked for ideas on ways in which they could assist at home.

In summary, the following generalizations can be made about parents of students in the advanced group: (1) they valued education for their children and encouraged them to do well at school; (2) common to these families was the bilingual preschool experience in which the teacher had trained parents to work with their children in the home and to communicate with the school; (3) parents in this group frequently read storybooks to their children; (4) the students were allowed to be independent in determining the organization of their daily homework routine; (5) parents checked for homework completion even if they had not directly assisted the student; and (6) parents initiated communication with teachers to clarify their children's progress.

Homework Literacy Interaction of Novice Readers

Most parents of children with novice reading ability took few opportunities to read largely because of a feeling of inadequacy in literacy skills. Verbal interaction between parents and children centered on day-to-day routines which often provided the opportunity for parents to encourage children to value school. Occasionally parents talked to their children about special family events in which they engaged. As did advanced readers, most of these children spent a great deal of time on their homework. However, these students' efforts were less successful than their advanced reader counterparts. A larger quantity of workbook pages and ditto sheets came home in the folders of the novice readers. This difference might be due to the fact that students in the novice reading groups often did not complete all of their skill exercise pages in the classroom and the teachers sent the work home. Parents tried to provide highly structured rules for children to follow when doing their homework. For example, they insisted that the children do homework at a designated time — before dinner after playing outside for a while; the children then had to sit, usually at the kitchen table, to work with a parent. In cases where parents assisted their children directly, they assumed that their role was to provide the answer.

Children in this group spent between half an hour and two hours on their assignments. Parents tried to help by sitting with the children for a while and helping with answers. In spite of this assistance, many of the students could not complete their homework. The following demonstrates how one mother helped her daughter, Norma. Although Norma completed this homework assignment, she and her mother failed to understand the goal of the activity which was to identify the book's author and locate the name in the appropriate space in the sheet.

(Just before dinner Norma sat at the dinner table and her mother stopped fixing dinner long enough to show her how to fill in the reading worksheet she had to complete.)

Mother: Sí, mi hija ahorita te ayudo. [Yes, dear, I'll help you right now.] (Mother sat down with Norma at the kitchen table and began to work with her.) ¿A ver, qué tienes que hacer? [Let's see what you have to do.]

Norma: ¿Qué es un personaje? [What's a character?]

M: A ver, el personaje es . . . (The mother looked at the book cover.) [Let's see the character is . . . .] (The mother continued to look at the book cover and pointed to the illustrator's name and comments to Norma.) Yo creo que esta es la persona que necesitas. [I think this is the person you need.] Espera, no es. [Wait that isn't it.]

(Norma watched as her mother continued to search for the author of the book. Her mother looked at the book cover and found the book title with the name 'Zorro' written in small letters at the bottom. She told Norma that this was the person who wrote the book.)

M: Aquí está. Este es él que escribió el libro. (She points to the book title). [This is it. Here is the one who wrote the book.]

(Norma proceeded to write the book title in the space that called for the name of the author.)

Like other parents in this group, this mother attempted to help her child with the homework questions. She felt it was her responsibility to give her child the answers in order to get good reports from the teacher. This same parent, however, expressed a sentiment which was common among this group of parents — frustration because of a lack of the skills necessary to understand the nature of the homework task.

These parents often underestimated the degree to which their children were underachieving. They believed the teacher when the child was not doing well, but when the teacher reported improvement, the parents understood that to mean grade level work and therefore that the problem of underachievement had been overcome. The parents possessed only vague notions about the criteria for their children's achievement; this was often further confused by the teacher's written weekly report to them and the occasional grade that appeared on homework papers. There was confusion between the grade on the homework and the student's overall performance. There was a general feeling of helplessness on the part of this group of parents. Often parents were not aware of alternatives available to them, such as contacting the teacher or someone else to help them in solving their children's academic problems.

In summary, the following generalizations can be made about parents of students in the novice group: (1) parents valued schooling and verbally encouraged their children to do their best; (2) they did not read frequently to their children; (3) the parents had not received any systematic training; (4) parents generally regulated their children's homework time and place, and assisted them by giving them the answer; (5) parents often blamed school failure on their children or on themselves; and (6) parents tended not to communicate with teachers about their children's achievement when they received negative reports from the school or when they observed their children having problems with their homework.

Comparison between Families of Advanced and Novice Readers

All of the parents were very interested in their children's school success and all of them assisted in their children's schoolwork in some form. Many, however, did not have access to the appropriate 'schema of literacy', that is, what literacy meant and how it was taught in the classroom, or of specific strategies to promote their children's literacy development. The who, what, where, when and why of the activity setting showed that parents' limited English skills restricted their ability to deal with English tasks. Although the parents had a limited understanding of the school's expectations, they were motivated to assist their children by facilitating completion of homework and encouraging academic success.

Parents believed, as did the teachers, that the children could improve their academic performance if parents helped the children more at home.

The parents, however, lacked the necessary skills with which to accomplish the goal. Regardless of the differences in literacy-related parent–child interactions among families, they shared commonalities: (1) all parents expressed an interest in having their children succeed in school; and (2) parents reminded their children about the need to apply themselves in school so they could improve their employment possibilities in the future.

Parents participated differently with their children on homework literacy tasks, although the majority shared a feeling of confusion as a result of unclear school expectations and vagueness about the meaning of the homework. Feelings of incompetence in their inability to help their children perpetuated a sense of isolation among the families. They felt responsible for their children's failure. The feeling of shame about being poor and lacking formal educational skills restricted their use of school and community resources. Whether the parents blamed themselves, their children or the teachers, the assignment of blame, as Varenne and McDermott (1986) note, tended to shift away from the institution to the individual. This means that training efforts directed at parents need to address this perception of responsibility for failure.

An explanation of the differential interaction practices in home literacy tasks suggests that in the homes where children have more independence in the way that they perform their homework, parents began very early to socialize children into independent behavior. That is, cultural practices do not appear overnight. Parental involvement in the interaction tasks exemplifies skills taught by the preschool teacher or acquired through contact with other school personnel.

Parents supported their children in homework in Spanish and sometimes in English, but they indicated that they participated less in their children's schooling as the students began to do their academic work only in English. Part of the problem that undermined the parents' feeling of competence was the nature of homework literacy activities. Decontextualized exercises and practice tasks made parental assistance difficult. Such tasks were dependent on subject matter knowledge covered in the classroom. Assignments reflected literacy as separate isolated skills to be mastered individually by drill and practice. They seldom encouraged higher level cognitive and language interaction between parents and children.

The school operated in the belief that students had to practice what they learned in the classroom. Thus the topic of homework literacy activities provides a vehicle to learn about the knowledge which children brought home from school. It describes what students learned in school and what they needed to know about school to be competent in the classroom. Insights on homework activities provide a means to understand what Mexican children knew about dealing with schools in Portillo.

Summary

This chapter has shown how the ability to handle text is learned through socially constructed behavior in which the teacher, student and parents have defined roles (Cook-Gumperz, 1986; Erickson, 1984). Teachers shaped classroom literacy activities through social interaction. In spite of the teachers' lack of adequate materials, administrative support and parental involvement, they had the freedom to design literacy activities in a way that they believed would best accomplish their goal. Most of the time teachers relied on the teachers' manual to present reading and writing lessons for both advanced and novice readers. Although students in advanced reading groups seemed to receive fewer rote memorization exercises than the novice readers, the discussion of textbook stories directed at students in both groups lacked not only higher order thinking skills but application of the knowledge in such a way as to incorporate the students' sociocultural experience out of school. The literacy activities usually inhibited students' participation by relegating discussion to a level of prescribed fact-based questions. These activities were repeated in homework assignments.

Home literacy activities consumed a great deal of time and effort for students and parents, and they relied largely on student recall skills to fill the blanks on worksheets or to practice memorizing vocabulary. According to McDermott, Goldman and Varenne (1984), these activities are but symbolic representations of real learning. In spite of the nature of homework literacy assignments, parents attempted to help their children in different ways. Differences in the way that parents and children completed the homework tasks illustrated the parents' differential ability to provide assistance. Some parents who did not understand the subject matter spent a great deal of time with the child, searching for the answer and ultimately giving an answer which might or might not be correct. More students in the advanced group were allowed autonomy in organizing their time, space and the completion of the task itself, and parents only monitored task completion. This practice shows that these parents had trained their children to be independent learners. Yet one could claim that their advanced placement in school also contributed to the students' success in the home since they received less homework and read assignments faster while novice readers received poor reports and consequently suggested to the parents more structure in homework activities.

In spite of the support they provided, all parents indicated that they felt inadequate in helping their children with schoolwork. Parents of students in both the advanced and the novice groups felt isolated because they wanted to help their children, but most of the time they did not know how to do so. Few of them contacted the teachers to inquire about their children's progress or to learn how to assist their children.

The practices of parents of advanced readers affirmed the thesis that Mexican children can succeed when the home and school share common goals and educational activities. Many parents of novice readers had not yet learned how schools in the United States operated, nor did they understand their role in their children's schooling. Assignments reflected literacy as separate, isolated skills to be mastered individually by drill and practice.

The role of teachers and parents in the acquisition of literacy provides a window through which we can observe students' knowledge about literacy as it relates to what they know about school, about classroom competence and about home activities related to school. Home literacy activities further illustrate how effectively children and parents obtain resources outside school for academic work that help them succeed in school. The data in this chapter illustrate that the path to students' learning must be a two-way street, with teachers acknowledging students' home culture and parents' participating in their children's schooling by learning about student activities in the classroom.

Chapter 7

Understanding the School's Communication

Mexican parents' participation in schools presents a controversial topic for many educators in Portillo schools because the latter report a lack of participation on the part of Mexican parents in comparison to Anglo parents. This tends to create communication problems between the schools and the Mexican families.

The fact that many working-class Mexican families with limited English proficiency lack access to the school system results in student underachievement and high dropout rates (Brown *et al.*, 1980; Rumberger, 1983, 1987). Problems pertaining to parental and student access to school resources have many sources. One possible explanation is that schools have a particular culture that caters to the White mainstream population (Spindler, 1955, 1982; Trueba, 1987). Successful participation requires that parents, as well as children, know what services are available and how to use them.

Families hold a great deal of power over their children where school matters are concerned. Studies show that parent participation in schools is linked to student academic achievement (Comer, 1984; Griffore and Boger, 1986). This makes it imperative to understand how the Mexican families in this study involved themselves in the schools and the role of the schools in encouraging the parents to participate.

To participate actively in the schools, Mexican parents must become informed about the school system and how it functions, their parental rights in obtaining information about their children, and their parental responsibilities for supporting their children through school. The concept of parent participation holds that informed parents play an important role in socializing children to participate meaningfully in school by learning the sociopolitical rules of the school. Active parents usually act as advocates on behalf of their children, providing more opportunity for their rights to be acknowledged in any conflict in school. The role parents exercise can be linked to that of a mentor who assists another to understand the culture of the school.

Research indicates that an important reason for many students to stay in school rather than to drop out is the parents' ability to intervene on behalf of the student (Delgado–Gaitan, 1988). Parent contacts and activities in the schools require sociocultural knowledge on the part of parents: to know the protocol for asking questions of school authorities, the type of questions to ask at the appropriate time, and appropriate personnel to contact in the school. Therefore, parents' participation in schools has to be considered in terms of the school's efforts to involve them.

The bilingual teachers in Portillo unanimously agreed on the importance of parental participation to student achievement. Most of the teachers reported that they usually had a high rate of parent involvement during parent-teacher conferences and yearly open house activities. However, there was an absence of daily parent-teacher contact in the schools.

The parents unanimously believed that education was important, and they agreed on the need to communicate with the schools. Most of them reported that they tried to attend open house and parent conferences. However, most also recognized that other than on those occasions they seldom contacted their child's teacher. Some families interacted in literacy activities in the home with their children but had minimal contact with the teacher. Other families did not read to their children at home but held their children accountable for completing their academic tasks and they frequently communicated with the teacher about their children's academic performance. Still other parents did not communicate frequently with the teacher but attempted to help their children with their school-related tasks because, according to teacher reports, their children were underachieving.

Parents defined success for their children in academic and social terms. They expected their children to receive excellent grades and to cooperate with teachers and classmates. Parents in the study participated in a variety of ways in their children's schooling, resulting in different levels of parental contact with the school. There tended to be two main approaches: parents acted on the weekly student reports, or parents tended to accept the teacher's report about their child.

Table 9 presents interview data on types of parent participation over eight months. Some parents were more directly involved with the school. They intervened in their children's school problems in activities beyond those conventionally seen as areas for parent involvement; others accepted the school as the final authority and maintained minimal contact

Table 9   Type and Frequency of Contact during an Eight-month Period between the School and the Twenty Parents of Students in the Two Reading Groups

Type of contact	Advanced (9)	Novice (11)
Weekly teacher reports	9	11
Reports sole contact with school	1	1
Teacher reports inconsistent with student performance	3	9
Attended bi-annual teacher conferences	8	8
Conferences sole contact with school	1	3
Teacher talks to parents vs. discussing with them	4	8
Parents initiate additional contact with teacher regarding student problem	6	2
No personal contact with teacher; would like to meet with teacher, but claim language barrier	1	5

with the school regarding their children's academic and social adjustment. Some parents' belief in their children's ability to learn motivated them to do everything they could to help them succeed in school.

Teacher Perceptions of Parental Involvement

The second and third grade teachers perceived that academic achievement was related to parental involvement to the extent that students of parents who frequently communicated with teachers were harder working. About a student in the middle reading group, the teacher commented, 'She tries hard. Even though she's still not in the advanced group, she's improved a lot. When she first came to my class she was in the novice group, but her mother started helping her and she was always sending me notes to make sure I sent homework. Now I'm really proud of her. I wish all parents were so cooperative.' While this child was perceived as a good student as a result of her mother's support, others were perceived to be intelligent but not as hard-working as a result of infrequent communication on the part of the parents. A teacher remarked about a boy who was in the novice group, 'He's really very intelligent but his mother is so overprotective that he doesn't think he has to do much work. If the mother would only push him more, he'd be more advanced in his reading.

The teacher expressed compassion about the parents' inability to help their children as much as Anglo mainstream parents could. She was aware of the long hours of work and the lack of literacy skills that prevented them from assisting their children in academic tasks. However, the teacher was adamant about the fact that parents should care and try to encourage their children to do their best in school. On this issue the teacher noted, 'It really makes a difference when the parents read my notes about their student's progress and send me notes. I feel like I can count on them to push on their end.' According to the teacher, parent communication was expected by the teacher and deemed necessary for the students' academic success. School rules and norms regarding the parents' role comprise a cultural expectation that differs from the experience of many Mexican parents. This was especially true for those parents who immigrated from rural areas, where schooling was not accessible to them. Schools in Mexico require parents to participate in monthly meetings with teachers regarding their children's educational needs, such as supplies and curriculum, and parents who came from urban areas in Mexico had the experience of attending school meetings. Some parents in Portillo, however, attended only through fourth grade in a rural school and they were accustomed to the teacher visiting them to recruit students for the rural schools. At present, however, even rural schools require parents to attend monthly meetings. For the immigrant Mexican families, participating in the school is a new practice and needs to be treated as a skill to be taught to parents.

Parents and Teacher Meet

The most common way in which parents demonstrated the value they placed on schooling was by participating in the annual open house activities in their children's school. Although most parents attended the event and enjoyed meeting the teachers, they felt that the event did not offer sufficient time to discuss their children's progress. Teachers recognized that the event was not designed for lengthy conferences. They did, however, consider the open house a manifestation of parental interest in their children's work because part of the event includes a display of children's most outstanding classwork.

The parent–teacher conferences provided another opportunity for parents to demonstrate an interest in their children's schooling. The schools attempted to schedule conferences with parents at a convenient hour since many parents work long hours. When a parent–teacher conference coincided with work-time most parents requested permission to leave work without pay to attend the meeting with the teacher. Some parents had to reschedule for a time in the late afternoon because their employers did not allow them to leave work. According to the teachers, the twenty minutes allowed for a parent–teacher conference seemed adequate for reporting on student performance. However, parents complained that the time allocated was barely enough to begin discussion of the students' learning problems. Both teachers and parents expressed major frustration in cases where students were underachieving and needed a great deal of additional support outside school. This was an issue for which the restricted parent-teacher conference time did not permit substantive discussion, much less resolution. The second grade teacher believed that since the parent-teacher conferences were so brief, maybe parents should visit the classroom more often and inform themselves about their children's progress. 'After all', she noted, 'I also send home weekly reports.' The third grade teacher commented, 'It's such a short time to try and explain to parents how important it is to help their child who is so far behind and you just know that they don't know what to do and I can't possibly do it in just a few minutes.' Nano's parent, Mr Ibarra, conveyed his frustration about the lack of time to ask questions when one does not understand the problem.

> Durante esas conferencias tenemos tan poco tiempo para comprender cuál es el problema que tiene Nano que salimos más confundidos que cuando entramos, porque tampoco nos dicen cómo es equ debemos ayudarle. Sólo nos dicen que debemos de ayudarle, pero uno no sabe. Y luego le preguntamos a la maestra y nos dice que debemos hacerlo que lea. Pues ya lo hacemos, así es que salimos en la misma. [During these conferences, we have such little time to understand Nano's problem and we leave more confused than when we walked in because they don't tell us how to help him. They just tell us that we should help him, but we don't know how (to do it). When we ask the teacher, she tells us that we should make him read. Well we already do that so that we end up in the same place.]

Teachers and parents found bi-annual conferences helpful in cases where the children were achieving well because they did not have to explain and discuss with the parents any student problems. In the cases of meetings with parents of children who were not performing at grade level, teachers and parents often felt that time was insufficient to do the problem justice. The concern about limited time for dealing with the student's learning problems points to a need for systematic parent education. Parents who expressed interest in helping their children felt that they were doing as much as they could, but often their children continued to fail in school. The issue of how to deal with children's persistent underachievement went unresolved during parent-teacher conferences. Communication between parents and teachers stagnated when teachers put the responsibility on parents and parents agreed to help as part of the solution, but often did not understand the nature of the problem. Usually parents who did not understand how and why their children did not improve academically blamed the child. Thus, while parent-teacher conferences helped some parents to understand their children's progress, it was not a viable forum for other parents to understand their children's lack of progress, especially if it meant that they had to work with their child at home. The limited time for parent-teacher conferences also calls into question the teachers' limited knowledge about home activities and the organization of the home to accommodate the school's activities. That is, teachers' ignorance of the home culture and social practices caused them to make inappropriate recommendations and to hold unrealistic expectations of families; this lead to continual parent and teacher frustration without resolution of the child's academic problem. Teacher's knowledge about the families and their ability to understand what happens to the school tasks that go home must be a part of the curriculum if they expect parents to participate and support children's academic work.

Written reports about the student provided a more frequent means for teacher communication with the parent. Parents differed in the way they dealt with the teacher reports. Some parents read the report and accepted it at face value. Other parents felt that the reports were ambiguous and challenged them by going to the school to inquire about the contents. One parent illustrated this:

> Yo no pude aceptar que mi hijo leía tan bien como sus hermanos aquí en la casa, y cada semana me manda la maestra un reporte que me dice que el niño va muy bien pero que necesita practicar su lectura y que debemos leer con él. Está muy confuso eso. ¿Cómo va [él] pues? Así es que yo fui a hablar con ella [la maestra]. [I couldn't accept that my son read so well with his brothers here in the home and every week the teacher sent home a report that said that he was doing well but that he needed to practise his reading and that we needed to read with him. This is very confusing. How is he really doing? So I went to talk with her (the teacher).]

Other parents believed that school was important, but felt incompetent to change the situation when teachers reported that their children were not doing well. For example, 'Pues dice la maestra que necesita practicar su lectura más aquí en la casa. Yo digo que es porque no pone atención. Le gusta jugar mucho'. [Well, the teacher said that he needed to practise his reading more here at home. I think it's because he doesn't pay attention. He likes to play a lot.]

The decision to contact the teacher or not involved several factors: the extent to which parents believe in the school's authority, the extent to which they knew their children's ability and the extent to which they believed in their children's ability to perform differently than the school reported.

Accepting the School's Explanations

Eleven of the twenty families in the study had minimal communication and contact with the school. They did not initiate contact with the school, but they did attend the yearly teacher-parent conferences and open-house activities.

The teacher used homework as a way to check completion and to teach discipline and responsibility required in doing work outside class and returning it. Because feedback was seldom provided, the teacher often did not know whether the students understood the task or not. Thus the instructional routine continued in class and the child who read in the novice group received more of the same homework which had been the source of frustration, confusion and sense of failure. If the homework was not completed, the teacher sent a note home with the child, indicating that the child should spend more time completing the homework and suggested to the parents that they help their children to read at home.

Upon receiving the teacher's weekly report about the child's progress, the parents talked to the student as in this example:

> (Alicia hands her mother the teacher's weekly written report.)

Mother: ¿Y esto? [What's this?]

Alicia: Mi reporte. [My report.]
> (The report read that Alicia was doing very well in all her class work but needed to practise reading more at home.)

M: Dice que tienes que practicar lectura. [It says you need to practise reading.]

A: No sé que leer. [I don't know what to read.]

M: Pues eso no está bien. ¿Por qué no traes un libro de la escuela? [That's not right. Why don't you bring a book from school.]

A: Se me olvida. [I forget.]

M: Mi hijita, nosotros no tuvimos la oportunidad que tienen ustedes. Deben de aprovecharse y aprender todo lo que puedan. Si no saben algo, pregunten. Tu papá y yo les ayudamos en lo que podamos.[Dear, we didn't have the opportunity that you have. You should take advantage and learn all that you can. If you don't know something, ask. Your father and I can help you in whatever way we can.]

A: Pero no sé algunas palabras. [But I don't know how to read some words.]

M: Entonces tienes que pedirle a mi o a tu papá que te ayudemos. De ahora en adelante tienes que traer un libro de la escuela para que te pongas a leer antes de que te pongas a ver la televisión. [Well then you have to ask me or your father to help you. From now on you'll have to bring a book to read from school and you'll have to read it before you watch TV.]

(There was no follow-through in making Alicia bring a book home from school to read nightly. The parents continued to receive reports that indicated the need for Alicia to practise reading at home.)

Typically parents paid attention to the teacher's reports about the child's school achievement. They interpreted the reports as a true statement about the student's ability and attempted to correct the situation by imposing strict rules of behavior for doing homework assignments. Correcting a reading problem became a task the parent assumed to the best of her ability. Alicia's mothers resorted to reiterating suggestions made by the teacher and then placed the burden on the child. The real problem was that neither the child nor the parent had the skills to deal with Alicia's lack of motivation and low reading skills because it was unclear why she lacked motivation to read. The mother reminded the child the ask for assistance from the teacher, yet there did not appear to be any follow-through on the part of the parent to insure that this would occur.

The child's reading problem needed to be solved with assistance from the teacher and other competent school personnel. The teacher, however, expected the parents to deal with the child's problem by following her instructions to read to Alicia. The way that the teacher represented the problem ignored the complex set of skills required to deal with underachievement in reading. That children learn to read better when parents read to them at home is a commonly known fact (Griffiths and Hamilton, 1984; Leichter, 1974). In a Mexican community, however, there needs to be close communication between the school and the parents because many families do not possess the knowledge to work with their children academically as schools expect (Delgado-Gaitan, 1989b). Thus the issue of sociocultural incongruence between the home and the school is not addressed.

Challenging the School's Explanations

Children of parents who participated more actively at school usually read at grade level or above, with the exception of one who read one year below grade level. Nine of the twenty parents in the study initiated frequent contact with the school regarding their children's academic performance. Three types of parent-initiated communication with the teachers were observed: (1) questions regarding the teacher's report about the student's performance; (2) concerns about student discipline in school; and (3) requests about ways to help children at home.

Parents of children who had attended the Portillo bilingual preschool communicated more frequently with the school than those parents whose children did not attend. Whereas only three of the eight novice readers had attended the preschool, six of the seven middle readers and all the advanced readers had attended. The significance of this factor is the strong parent education program that the teacher conducted. The importance of communicating with the school about the curriculum and their child's performance was impressed on the parents. This monthly parent training motivated parents to overcome their fear and ignorance about the US school system and taught them to participate in their children's schooling.

At home, reminding students to pay attention in class, study hard and learn everything possible is frequently heard parental advice. This typical form of parental guidance was observed in all the families in the study. It was of particular significance that some of the parents believed it was necessary for them to insure that their verbal directions were carried out. They initiated contacts with the teachers regarding their children's assignments, their conduct and ways of supporting them at home.

Academic reports went home weekly with the students. For most members of the advanced groups, the reports were positive, with maybe one statement about the fact that the student should continue to study at home as well as review the multiplication tables. Some of the parents commented that they did not need to talk to the teacher because their children were good students. The majority of the parents commented to the child about the teacher's statements. 'Dice la maestra que tienes que estudiar tus tablas. No se te olvide. Qué bueno que siquiera sigues leyendo bien. Guárdalo para que se los enseñes a tu papá.' [The teacher says that you have to study your times tables. Don't forget. It's good that you're doing well in reading. Put it away so that you can show your father when he gets home.] The parents did not drop the issue at this point. Some of the parents walked the students to school the following Monday and talked briefly with the teacher before class began. The teacher welcomed the parents and asked them to sit down. Generally parents asked their children to stay and listen to the conversation.

A frequent interaction involved parents telling the teacher that they were concerned that their children learn the multiplication tables and requested materials from the school to help at home. The teacher usually complied by loaning the child a set of flashcards which could be checked out at the end of the day. Parents often reminded their children to bring the item home at the end of the day. 'Tú tienes que recordarle a la maestra que te dé las tarjetas, eh no se te olvide.' [You have to remind the teacher to give you the flashcards at the end of the day, OK don't forget.] Rarely did children forget to ask the teacher for materials to take home. On occasion students would start walking home and then return to school, running into the classroom breathlessly to pick up the materials. They were able to do this since the teachers usually worked late.

At the end of a few weeks students no longer needed to rely on their parents to request special materials for homework. They asked the teacher to loan them books, games, paper or any other props for home study. One of the students commented, 'Para mí es como un juego porque mi mamá me ayuda con mis estudios cuando llevo así otras materias y podemos hacerle como si fuera escuelita en la casa.' [For me it's like a game because my mother can help me with my studies when I bring home other materials and we can play school at home.] This student's enthusiasm was typical of many of the students in this classroom. The teacher fostered this attitude in class, and the parent's role reinforced the child's motivation to learn.

Although homework provided the most frequent motive for parental intervention, other concerns prompted parents to contact the school. Behavior problems and unfair disciplining resulted in frequent parental visits to the school. José, for example, was an advanced reader who had difficulty, as the teacher described it, 'keeping his hands to himself'. He was continually getting into trouble because children complained that he pushed them, hit them or touched them in some way that annoyed them. José always said that he was sorry and that he did not mean to do it. The teacher's weekly reports to the parents usually made some reference to his social conduct. José's mother typically went to meet the teacher in José's presence about twice a month. She sometimes took time off from work to deal with his discipline report. The teacher assured the mother that José was a nice person, tried hard to do good work, and most of the time got good grades in all his subjects, as evidenced by the fact that he was an advanced reader. His preoccupation with touching others was a concern for the parent who wanted her child to 'behave'. The mother continued to communicate with the teacher through notes and personal meetings. Finally, at the beginning of May the mother became annoyed that the teacher was only calling attention to José's behavior without any regard for the other children involved in the complaints against him. Her comments to the teacher in José's presence were:

> Usted tiene la responsabilidad de ver como los demás también toman parte en causar estos problemas. Yo no estoy convencida que solo mi hijo tenga la culpa. El siempre dice que no lo hace de adrede. El no es niño malo. Es bueno y no digo que es santo pero tampoco los demás son. A ver ¿por qué los demás se quejan tanto? Permítame hablar con ellos. Ahorita ya me tengo que ir a trabajar pero espero que tú, José, ya dejes de tocar a otros y si es verdad que ellos no quieren que los toques entónces no los toques a no ser que te den ellos permiso. [You have the responsibility to see how the rest also contribute to the problem. I'm not convinced that my son is the only one at fault. He always tells me that he's not doing it on purpose. He's not a bad boy. He's a good boy, I'm not saying he's a saint, but neither are the others. Let me see why the others complain so much. Let me talk with them. Right now I have to go to work but I expect that you, José, stop touching others and if it's true that they don't want you to touch them, then don't do it unles you ask them for permission.]

The boy looked confused and responded:

> Ellos dicen que yo los empujo, pero no es verdad. Sólo pongo mi mano así. [They say that I push them, but it's not true. I just put my hand like this.]
> Pues te digo que ya no quiero que se quejen de ti y tú solo vas a tocar a alguien si ellos te dan permiso de que los toques. ¿Entiendes?' [Well I'm telling you that I don't want them to complain about you anymore and you're only going to touch someone if they give you permission to touch them. Understand?]

Mrs Mata sat quietly for a few moments and then assured the parent that she was not passing false judgment against her son and that other children were treated equally and were also expected to keep their hands to themselves. The days that followed were uneventful, as José made every effort to avoid touching anyone. Then a few days later José was standing in line with other students and a boy ran up against him and pushed him and others in front. The children all looked at José and yelled, 'Stop it!' He quickly defended himself, 'Not me, it was him!' He pointed at the boy who stood behind him talking to his friends. The teacher came out to let the class in and found the children pointing fingers at each other. After her fact-finding questions, she commented to José 'José, recuerda lo que dijo tu mama.' [José, remember what your mother said.] The boy looked angry that he had been accused and walked into the classroom with the rest. He walked up to the teacher and told her in a soft voice,

> Yo sé que usted, maestra cree que yo los empuje allá afuera, pero no es cierto. Yo ya no hago esas cosas y no quiero que me sigan culpando por cosas que no hago. [I know you think I pushed the others out there, but I want you to know that I changed and that I don't do those things anymore and I don't want to be blamed for things that I don't do.]

The teacher ignored José's comment other than to tell him to sit down. José's self-assertion signaled that he had internalized his mother's expectations to the point that he no longer accepted his teacher's and classmates' false accusations. José's mother's intervention created changes for him in learning how to deal with the sociopolitical culture of the classroom. Whether or not José had initially been misbehaving is almost immaterial, because the teacher and classmates learned to scapegoat him to the extent that he could no longer defend himself. The mother's intervention was necessary to help José recognize that he had to take responsibility for his action, but that he also had to stand up for himself. José recognized his rights as a person and acquired the courage and skill to challenge and question. As a result, José understood the consequences of his own behavior and knew that he was acting according to the rules of the school. When he was wrongly assumed to be misbehaving, he knew to address the teacher as the authority and insist that he not be misjudged. The parent's intervention became a learning experience for José.

Many parents who made more frequent contact with the school and intervened on behalf of their children had received training when their children attended preschool. Eight of the children had not been to preschool in Portillo, thus the parents had not participated in the intense parent training. While this study does not intend to show a cause and effect relationship between parent training and student achievement, it does purport to show the process through which parents are socialized to communicate with schools. Given that the preschool and the migrant programs were established to serve the Spanish-speaking parents, it is important to understand the extent of their influence on the parents.

Preschool Parent Education

Parents of children in the Spanish language preschool became co-teachers with the teacher, Mrs Baca. She made it her goal to educate the parents about the preschool curriculum and about ways to design learning activities with their children at home. Parent education is a mandated regulation by the State Department funding agencies, and this teacher's efforts have proven to be particularly effective in engaging the Spanish-speaking parents to participate in their children's education.

Mrs Baca was a teacher in Colombia before imigrating to the United States. Her position as a preschool teacher afforded her the opportunity to teach in Spanish and to work with families in her own community. Beyond her language, cultural and community affiliation with these families, her teaching skills have won her national recognition. Bilingual experts like Cummins (1986) have observed her instruction. Mrs Baca organized her classroom with Spanish as the sole language of instruction in contexts where all children could interact with her and with their peers in meaningful experiential tasks. This made cognitive and language development inevitable due to the extensive use of the language in meaningful activities. This concept of learning through social interaction between the adult and child was taught to parents at their monthly meetings. Each month was dedicated to a specific topic selected by the parents such as 'learning through cooking' or 'disciplining with care'.

The teacher used daily tasks at home to provide examples for parents to involve children and to make the activity a learning one. For example, during one session Mrs Baca used the task of making potato salad to illustrate appropriate ways to involve children.

> (Mrs Baca addressed a group of about forty-five parents on a Friday evening. She first reported on the successful field trip to the Los Angeles Science Museum and thanked those parents who participated in the excursion. She then described the type of lessons that children received during the week, including making a potato salad. She told them that she would show them how they could involve children in similar learning activities at home.)

T: Pueden ustedes poner a los niños que les ayuden a preparar una ensalada de papa. Muchas veces ustedes piensan que es más fácil hacer un projecto sin los niños porque están de prisa y piensan que los niños les estorban. La realidad es que siempre es mejor que los niños tomen parte en las actividades de la casa porque pueden aprender mucho. Aquí tenemos todos los ingredientes que muchos de ustedes usan en su cocina. Los niños en la clase prepararon una ensalada con sus propias manitas y yo les voy a enseñar cómo ustedes pueden usar esta actividad en sus casas de modo que los niños aprendan de ustedes. [You can get your children to assist you in preparing a potato salad. Often you think that it's easier for you to carry out your work without your children because you're in a hurry and you think that your children get in the way. The reality is that it is better that you involve your children in your daily activities because they learn a great deal. Here were have many of the same ingredients that you use in your home to make potato salad. Students in class prepared a potato salad in class with their own little hands and I'm going to show you how you can have the children help you with the same activity in your home in a way that they can learn from you.

(Mrs Baca proceeded to demonstrate step by step how to prepare a potato salad while the parents observed. The instructional activity focused on the language that parents needed to use with their children, as illustrated in the following example.)

T: (She had a preschool child assisting her in the activity.) Nati, por favor pásame las papas que estan en el olla. Mira el pellejo, esto se tiene que quitar. Después de que le quitemos ese pellejo a las papas, que crees que tenemos que hacer con las papas? [*Nati, please pass me the potatoes in that bowl. Look at the skin, this has to be removed. After we remove the skin from the potatoes, what do yo think we have to do to them?*]

(Following the demonstration parents asked questions about the use of sharp utensils with young children. Mrs Baca encouraged parents to teach children how to use household equipment because they're less likely to get hurt if they are taught proper usage.)

This example illustrates how Mrs Baca focused on specific language use while involving children in daily home activities. Her goal was to have parents observe how to share a cooking experience with their children. She helped the parents learn that their daily tasks provided a natural context in which they could be teachers. This type of parent education activity gave parents ideas on ways to interact with their children in the home. Through Mrs Baca's open door policy in the preschool, she taught parents that visiting the classroom and participating in activities were critically important for both the child and the parent. She invited parents to visit the classroom whenever they came to leave or pick up their children. During those opportunities to observe their children, parents learned to inquire about their children's progress as well as what constituted a classroom lesson. Mrs Baca usually engaged them in discussion about their child's activity during the day. Therefore, whenever the teacher had any problems with the child in the classroom, she seldom encountered any difficulty in getting parents to cooperate with her. Her approach in dealing with parents resembled her caring nature with children, as demonstrated in the following classroom event:

> *T:* (She asked the parents to come and confer with her. She talked with the mother about the son's inability to follow directions in the last few days. The child was present.) Saúl ha tenido algunos problemitas estos días pasados. Su comportamiento indica que posiblemente tiene algo que lo está molestando y quisiera saber si tiene usted alguna información que me pudiera ayudar a comprender cómo puedo lidiar con él. Ya tiene tres días que no quiere cooperar con su grupo y yo quiero que sepan ustedes, con el niño aquí presente porque es muy importante que se sienta él a gusto con sus amiguitos. [Saul has had some problems during these past days. His behavior indicates that maybe something is bothering him and I would like to know what information you can give me to help me deal with him. For three days he has refused to cooperate with his group and I want you to know, with him present here, that it's important for him to feel comfortable with his little friends.]
> (The parent confided to Mrs Baca that Saul might be experiencing some emotional conflict because his father had to leave for Mexico to attend his mother's funeral.)

Mrs Baca used her relationship with the parents to obtain information which she used to work more effectively with the children in the classroom. She raised a typical disciplinary problem to the level of a socially constructed learning activity. As a result of knowing that Saul's father had to leave for Mexico, Mrs Baca felt that she could talk with him and help him feel more comfortable and safe. Mrs Baca used activities like group discussions to talk about traveling to Mexico to visit relatives. This provided an opportunity for children to share their experiences and feel more supported. Mrs Baca's ability to turn a child's difficult situation into a social interaction activity for learning illustrates her talent in co-teaching with parents.

Migrant Parent Education

Parents who worked in the migratory-related industries, including agricultural and fishing jobs, could participate in the School District's Migrant Education Program. Nearly 100 families, all Spanish-speaking, belonged to the program. Their children received special tutorial services from school bilingual paraprofessionals and the parents received health benefits for the family. Part of the Migrant Program also required the director to meet with the parents three or four times a year to inform them of program activities and to provide information pertaining to social needs, such as immigration rights and public health counseling on alcoholism. The director made an effort to schedule speakers for the parent meetings. On average between twenty and fifty parents attended. The program included childcare because attendance was required and the director believed that most parents would make an effort to attend if they had assistance with childcare.

Meetings began with a presentation by the director about important school activities. For example, during the time that the School District programs were being evaluated by the State Department of Education compliance officers, the director described the process to the parents and explained that they should attend the parent meetings which would be scheduled by the compliance team so that they could discuss concerns and expectations with them. One parent, Mrs Alonzo, asked, 'Y los oficiales hablan español o van a tener interpretes para nosotros?' [Do the officials speak Spanish or will they have translators for us?] The director responded, 'Pues, creo que uno de los miembros del equipo es bilingue, pero yo también voy a estar allí y si no, voy a asegurar que tengan a alguien que interprete para ustedes.' [Well, I think that one of the members of the team is bilingual, but I'll be there too and if not, I'll be sure to have a translator there.] However, none of the parents from the Migrant Program attended the meetings with the compliance officers. Two of the paraprofessionals in the program were present.

The presentations made by invited members of community agencies typically informed parents about specific problems. Speakers were usually selected by the director, who asked the parent for their approval. They always accepted the director's recommendation. Although these presentations did not train parents, the information delivered to the families was usually thought to be important. A parent, Mr Sanchez, commented that he was not interested in all of the topics which guests presented because only some pertained to his family's needs, but he added, 'Yo pienso que todo esto es muy importante para alguien porque no es posible que todo sea de interes para todos. Pero aúnque no nos sirva ahorita aquí a la mejor más allá puede servir a mi familia.' [I think that everything is very important for somebody because it's not possible that everything be of interest to everyone. But even if it doesn't help us right now, maybe later on it'll help my family.]

Problems expressed by some of the parents were not so much about relevance of the presentations but about the decision-making process used to decide on the type of parent education for the group. Usually the parents were asked to vote on their choice, as presented by the director. A majority vote decided whether or not the guest speaker would be invited. Parents typically did not challenge the director's suggestion. One of the problems of this approach to parent education was that it failed to provide follow-up on the issues raised. Although parents might find the presentations helpful, they usually did not change their home activities or behavior as a result. Such changes require more consistent training, with thorough discussion on the topic to inform participants about ways of applying it.

One of the topics covered in these presentations to Migrant Education parents was the type of contacts that parents made with school personnel. The director provided the parents with a list of bilingual school personnel they could contact to deal with concerns about their children. One of the issues raised by parents in the Migrant Program was the need for parents who were more experienced in dealing with schools to organize themselves in order to help other parents.

School Workshops and Advisory Committees

Parents find it easier to communicate verbally with staff in elementary than in high schools. The elementary schools have more bilingual personnel with whom the parents can relate. In spite of the availability of bilingual personnel, communicating with the school became a problem for many Spanish-speaking parents because many written memos were not translated into Spanish, especially for students in the upper elementary grades, including the junior high school. One of the principals admitted that she was negligent in sending memos home in Spanish, but she explained that professional bilingual personnel had very restricted time and the paraprofessionals had minimal Spanish literacy skills. That they did not receive school newsletters and other memos in Spanish concerned most of the Spanish-speaking parents; they felt that they were systematically excluded from learning about their children's activities in school. One parent expressed her frustration in the following way:

> Me parece a mí que si es importante que yo sepa de lo que están haciendo mis niños en la escuela y cómo es que yo debo de participar entonces debe la escuela considerar que todo eso se tiene que comunicar en el idioma que yo comprendo. Y claro lo que me dice esto es que no les importa que yo participe. [It seems to me that if it's important for me to know what my son is doing in school and how it is that I'm supposed to participate in the school, then the school should consider the fact that all of that (information) has to be communicated to me in a language that I understand. Clearly, what this communicates to me is that my participation is not important.]

The communication gap between parents and school created a great deal of resentment on the part of Spanish-speaking parents. At the same time the school stood in judgment of the parents for not communicating with the school.

The parent education component in the schools has a rather miniscule role in overall education plans. Although school level parents workshops were planned on topics like 'Reading to Children' and 'Effective Disciplining in the Home', they usually occurred only once during the school year and provided for little or no follow-up. That is, parent education exists in isolation from the rest of the parents' role in the school. In Maple School four workshops were offered on 'Effective Discipline' as a part of the parent education component of the school plan. The workshops were offered in English and Spanish. Attendance in the two groups was comparable. Thirty parents started the series and about fourteen completed it. Spanish-speaking parents who attended the workshops felt that they gained something and expressed their desire to see more Mexican parents present. That this was the only school that offered workshops for any parents showed the low priority that the issue of systematic parent education has in Portillo. Mr Clark, Director of Special Projects, observed that historically parent education workshops have attracted minimal participation, even by Anglo parents.

The State Department of Education requires elementary schools to submit a plan to use state and federal funds in several instructional and training components, including parent education. Within each school staff have to develop a plan for training parents. Generally the school parent advisory committee has an input into the type of activities which become part of the yearly school plan. Spanish-speaking parents, however, seldom participated in the advisory committees because meetings were held in English and translation was seldom provided. Even on occasion when translation was available, the bureaucratic language about budgets and curriculum was cumbersome to translate. Furthermore, Spanish-speaking parents found it difficult to comprehend the type of decisions in which they were expected to participate. This indicates the specialist skills required by parents to participate in decision making. One parent, Mrs Hernandez, complained about her attendance at a school advisory meeting after receiving a notice in English:

> Yo le pedí a mi hijo que me ayudara a leer el aviso que llegó tocante a esa junta del comité de padres de la escuela Marina. La reunión era a las tres de la tarde. Pues, ¿cuántos padres pueden asistir a esa hora? Yo fui porque había tomado parte del diá para ir con el doctor y me tocó que salí temprano a tiempo para asistir la junta. Resulta que yo fui la única persona mexicana y la reunión fue toda en inglés. Con lo poco de inglés que comprendo parece que les iban a dar $100.00 a cada maestra pero no sé de dónde era que sacaban ese dinero ni para qué era el dinero. Sentí mucho coraje que no podía entender todo. ¿Qué puede una hacer cuando pasa eso? [I asked my son to help me translate the memo that arrived about the meeting of parents of Marina School. The meeting was at three in the afternoon. Well, what parent can attend at that hour? I went because I had taken part of the day off to go to the doctor and I got our early in time to attend the parent meeting. It turns out that I was the only Mexican person there and the meeting was all in English. It took all of the few words in English that I know to understand that they were making a decision on $100 that they were going to give each person, but I couldn't understand where the money was coming from and what it was going to be used for. I was terribly angry that I couldn't understand everything. What can one do in a situation like that?]

Mrs Hernandez's situation illustrates an alienating experience. She found herself at a meeting she had been invited to attend, but she could not understand the purpose of the event. Her question at the end indicates that she was at a loss about what to do in similar situations and wanted to know how to deal with such circumstances.

The problem of Spanish-speaking parents participating in schools has its roots in institutions that expect parent activism without communicating with parents in their own language. To expect parents to participate in the school's decision-making process, without using the parents' language and without acquainting them with the way the school functions, poses an obvious obstacle in communication between Mexican parents and the schools. The system of parent advisory committees was established to meet federal and state regulations in a manner that was convenient to school personnel. Typically the school site parent committee was not seen as a forum in which to educate parents about the organization of the school if they did not already have some understanding of the system.

Summary

The school, in general, either invites and encourages parents to participate or gives the message that they are not welcomed. If Mexican parents are to participate on behalf of their children, schools need to reach the parents through their own language, informing them of the protocols of the school, and legitimately working with them to resolve their children's problems.

The school culture in Marina School dictated that parents actively participate in school, both by inquiring about students' achievement and by assisting at home with school-related tasks. The problem was that some of the Mexican families were more proficient than others. This resulted in unequal participation and perpetuated inequity for children.

Most of the families in the study had good relationships with the teachers and the school largely due to the bilingual abilities of school personnel. Diverse levels of parental intervention in their children's schooling existed among the Mexican families in Portillo. The kind of involvement depended on the parents' knowledge of the school system and their beliefs about their own role in their children's schooling.

Communicating with the school was second nature for some parents but seemed useless to others. The more active parents expressed a view of the school as a place where their children could learn, and if there were any problems that prevented their children from accomplishing their goal, the parents would take action. Perhaps the word 'goal' provides a clue to what constituted the difference between the two groups of families. Goal direction provides families with a framework from which to view the school and organize themselves. There was an implicit trust in the children's abilities and a perception of the institution as the provider of a service. Thus, if any problems occurred, parents acted without hesitation to resolve them. As a result, children also learned about the services available to them. This approach to dealing with the system differed from that of parents who felt powerless as a result of their limited formal schooling.

Powerlessness describes a consistent feeling among the less active parents as well as among many active parents who did not get adequate results from the school when they intervened on behalf of their children, as in the case of José reported above. While all parents sincerely believed in the importance of schooling, many believed that the children's lack of motivation (as well as their own lack of literacy skills) accounted for their children's underachievement problems at school. If the children were unsuccessful at school, they believed that it was the children's fault. Parents felt powerless to deal with many of the children's academic problems because of their own limited formal schooling.

Parents are capable of assisting children in learning to obtain resources from the school and asking questions of the teacher when they are taught to participate in schools. Parental intervention directly assisted children in school achievement. Other children, however, were not being assisted by their parents due to the parents' lack of training and feeling of isolation and powerlessness. Many of these children were in the novice reading groups. This is not to suggest that children who are in low reading groups experience academic problems simply because their parents do not act as advocates for them. The data here, however, suggest that many of these children have internalized a self-perception that they are slow learners and that their learning problems are their fault. When parents do not intervene to investigate children's underachievement or to find material resources to help their children, misperceptions about the student's self and external motivation are likely to occur. Thus parental intervention to interrupt the students' negative sense of self or to prevent it from occurring becomes even more critical.

The role of parent training programs is significant. These must be designed to address the issue of parental involvement in children's schooling. As parents learn how to gain access to the school system, they can guide their children through school in a way that provides knowledge and direction for them to learn how to be independent learners.

The preschool parent education component played a key role in teaching parents about the school culture. This suggests the need for well organized parent education programs and networks that can teach parents about the school system and help them to maximize their role as teachers. The gap in Portillo schools existed in the absence of systematic parent education for Spanish-speaking parents after children left preschool. This study revealed a pressing need for an organized structure to incorporate parents and to provide a vehicle through which they can work collectively to learn about the school system and ways of supporting their children through school.

Chapter 8

Redefining Parents' Role in the Schools

A Spanish-speaking parent organization in Portillo evolved through several stages that represented parental efforts to engage in dialogue about their children's needs. Research on how Spanish-speaking parents participated in their children's education in and out of school with respect to literacy acquisition revealed that parents pursued various avenues to inform themselves about schooling in Portillo and help their children with school-related tasks in the home. One path which parents followed was to organize themselves into a leadership group through which they would socialize each other about how to communicate with the schools. Four phases of action characterized the negotiations from isolation through to the formation of a district Spanish-speaking representative committee: building awareness, mobilization, motivation and fear, commitment and district response.

Social Isolation

Social isolation from other families in respect to school matters created a knowledge gap for many Spanish-speaking parents. Most had not learned the meaning of participating in a system which required different sociocultural knowledge and practices from those they knew. This isolation fostered a feeling of helplessness for many parents who did not have the skills to communicate with the school as the school expected. Although some parents discussed problems related to their children's schooling among themselves, the concerns raised were not resolved. Parents shared experiences informally with each other about going to the school to talk with teachers and about other ways they used to alleviate the problem. However, most parents did not initiate contact with the school if their child had a problem. Either they were intimidated by the school and their limited English-speaking ability, or they did not know who in the school to contact. Generally they waited until school personnel contacted them. Mrs Ramos commented: 'No voy a la escuela porque casi no conosco a nadie allí y me da verguenza. Los maestros nos mandan reportes de Andrea y así nos damos cuenta cómo va en sus estudios.' [I don't go to the school because I don't know anyone there and I'm embarrassed. The teachers send me reports on Andrea and that way I stay informed about her progress.] Parents' fear of dealing with the schools was perpetuated by the lack of any formal organization that could provide an opportunity for networking with other parents who shared similar concerns. For parents who communicated more frequently with the schools, acting alone meant frustration; they continuously faced obstacles and there was no one to direct them to more appropriate sources. Such was Mrs Hernandez's experience:

> Recibí una nota de la maestra de mi niño en el primer grade. Me decía que no se estaba portando bien [en la clase] y que teníamos que hablar con él. Pues lo hicimos y le dijimos que tenía que portarse bien y respetar la maestra y a los otros niños. Luego en dos días llegó mi hijo de la escuela y le pregunté cómo le había ido en el paseo donde iba la clase. Me sentí como que me habían arrancado mi corazón cuando me dijo que la maestra le había dicho que él no podía ir porque no se había portado bien. La maestra no le había dicho nada tocante a que no lo iba dejar ir. Se me hizo tan feo que fui a hablar con la mastra pero ya no estaba allí y no supe que hacer. Luego ya era el fin delaño y se acabó la escuela. Hasta este punto no sé porque hizo eso la maestra. [I received a note from my son's first grade teacher. She said that he wasn't behaving (in class) and that we should talk to him. Well we did and told him that he had to behave and respect his teacher and his classmates. Two days later when my son came home, I asked him about his field trip. I felt like they had ripped out my heart when he told me that the teacher told him that he could not go on the trip because he had misbehaved. The teacher hadn't even told him that he wasn't going on the trip. I thought what the teacher did was so terrible that I went to talk with her but she wasn't there and I didn't know what to do. Then it was the end of the year and the school was over. So I still don't know why she did what she did.]

When Mrs Hernandez received the note from her child's teacher, she followed through with the request to talk with her son. She then assumed that her son's behavior had improved. She had no clue that it would affect something as important as his attendance on a field trip. Mrs Hernandez's anger motivated her to contact the teacher, but when her effort failed, she was at a loss about how to take further action. This was a common occurrence for many parents who were confronted by an unsuccessful effort and then became confused about the next step. In this case the situation was complicated by the end of the year and the teacher's leaving the building. She also reported not knowing that the principal could help her to solve the problem. Therefore, even parents who attempted to contact the school often failed to solve their problems because they did not have the knowledge to transcend unforseseen obstacles.

Those parents who did not participate as frequently in the school turned their lack of knowledge about school and fear of dealing with it on their children and blamed them for failing academically. Flor Cortina's parents commented on her academic problems in school:

> Tiene problemas con su lectura y la maestra nos manda reportes de que le ayudemos a leer, pero no le gusta. Yo creo que algunos niños son cabezones y tienen más problemas para aprender. [She has problems with her reading and the teacher sends home reports and tells us to help her read, but she doesn't like it. I think that some children have thick heads and they have more problems learning.]

Mrs Cortina believed that Flor's learning problems were terminal and felt helpless in attending to her needs when she received reports from the teacher. Her mother's decision not to intervene or inquire about ways to help Flor suggested a gap in awareness of how learning develops and of the parent's role in the process. The likely consequence will be continual learning problems for Flor until her classroom learning environment changes to accommodate her home experience and/or until her mother can learn how to intervene on her behalf.

Awareness of Rights

Awareness in the context of parent education refers to the Spanish-speaking parents' consciousness of their social environment and the conditions under which they operate. Achieving this awareness was facilitated by advocates in the schools. Parents became aware about the knowledge they needed to help their children. This phase preceded the parents' mobilization to organize themselves.

While Spanish-speaking Portillo parents varied in their knowledge about the schools, the majority lacked the resources to communicate with the school. Most parents agreed that they needed more information about school organization and their role as parents in their children's schooling. This awareness became more pronounced for many through meetings in which I as a researcher presented data on family literacy activities in the home and parental contact with the school. Parents recognized that they needed training to communicate with the school and to learn strategies to help their children with schoolwork at home.

Upon recognizing the need for further training, some parents requested the help of the migrant education director. They asked him to provide speakers who could address issues such as how to help children who have disciplinary problems in school, how to communicate with a teacher about children's reading problems and other concerns about children's education. Parents stated 'Necesitamos más información sobre estos temas para poder ayudarles a nuestros hijos.' [We need more information about these topics to be able to help our children.] The director listened to their requests and at subsequent meetings of the Migrant Education Program parents heard guest speakers speak about child abuse and AIDS. Although these were not topics that directly related to parent/teacher communication, the topics covered by representatives from community agencies helped to build consciousness about issues that affected some families.

Information sessions heightened parents' awareness of topics related to their children's education. However, parental awareness of the schooling process required a more comprehensive structure so that parents might integrate the information. Sessions involving guest speakers provided useful information for the families, but this had a low rate of carry-over into the daily lives of the parents. New information typically needs to be heard several times in various forms before it becomes part of regular routines and behaviors. Thus making parents aware of different aspects of their children's schooling had limited merit.

The awareness building sessions did provide a basis for parents to become acquainted with their needs and to begin thinking about ways of taking action. Many comments exchanged between parents indicated that they wanted to learn more about ways to participate in their children's education and they generally believed that the School District could provide it. One parent summarized what others had expressed, 'Todo esto que necesitamos saber es muy importante y deben de enseñarnos'. [All of this that we need to know is very important and they should show us.] In other words parents wanted the District to provide the necessary training. This desire was based on a lack of understanding of the school system, of their responsibility as parents and a lack of confidence in their own power. Furthermore, they did not know how to begin the process of organizing themselves.

Advocates like the director of Migrant Education and the bilingual preschool teacher played an important role in building awareness for Spanish-speaking parents. Cummins (1986) discussed the concept of advocates and concluded that in order for Mexican children to succeed in school, advocates had to play a crucial role for them and for their parents. In Portillo these key figures in the School District reached out to the families in ways that appealed to their needs through considering their language and cultural practices.

Mobilization

To embark on a voyage toward an unknown destination takes much courage and love. The parents' motivation grew out of knowing that nothing could be as difficult as continuing in isolation and ignorance. This was demonstrated in the action taken by one parent who suggested to others that they needed to get themselves organized in a group that could help those parents who did not have as much experience with the schools. His invitation was made during a meeting of the Migrant Education Program in which I had presented data about parents' participation in the schools. The parent, Mr Ramos, noted, 'Algunos de nosotros tenemos más conocimiento sobre estos temas y tenemos que organizarlos en un grupo para ayudarles a esas familias que no tienen la misma experiencia. Así nos ayudamos uno a otro.' [Some of us have more knowledge about this topic and we need to organize into a group to help other families who do not have as much experience. That way we can help each other.] Other parents did not immediately accept this particular invitation with enthusiasm. The Migrant Education director endorsed the idea but did not offer constructive direction on how to proceed. The idea might have been left dormant had it not been for my intervention as a researcher.

My decision to intervene as a researcher was based on the data which I had collected in the school, the homes and the parent meetings about parents' roles in their children's learning. Preliminary analysis of that data suggested that most Spanish-speaking parents did not have much experience with the schools and therefore could not participate actively in them. This analysis supported the need for a parent leadership group of those who had more skill and experience with the schools. Based on this assumption, I suggested to the person who had talked about the formation of a leadership group that he organize those parents whom he felt could help others. I established two major points to guide my participation.

1 As a researcher I would not initiate parents' organizational activities. Rather, I would serve only as a facilitator, available to parents about parent involvement, logistics for organizing and about families' needs and the School District's activities on the basis of the research data collected.

2 I would continue to collect data on the process of parent involvement as the Mexican parents organized themselves.

At the first meeting of the Spanish-speaking parents seven parents and myself were present. I explained that the idea for the meeting had been presented by Mr Ramos, who endorsed the need for a leadership group of parents who could assist others in becoming better acquainted with the school. Parents at the meeting unanimously supported the concept of organizing to share their experience with other parents who might not be as active in the schools. Mrs Ramos stated:

> Pues yo digo que la idea de organizarnos para apoyarnos es muy importante porque podemos entre todos ayudarnos uno al otro. Es decir pues yo no sé mucho de lo que se debe de saber tocante a nuestro niños. Uno hace lo más posible y muchas veces no es suficiente pero como lo veo entre todos podemos saber más y compartir y apoyarnos. [Well I think that the idea of organizing ourselves to support each other is a very important one because we can help each other. I mean, well, I don't know much about what we need to know regarding our children. I do the best I can and often that's not enough, but like I see it we can all know more and support each other.]

Parents exhibited a spirit of cooperation and enthusiasm for the notion of working together. Along with comments of support some parents raised questions about parent representation:

> Yo quiero saber si este groupo va hacer dicisiones para otros padres de familia porque es necesario que ellos tengan un voto en este grupo. En ese caso necesitamos tener una elección donde todos los padres de habla-español reconecen este grupo como representate de ellos. [I want to know if this group will be a decision-making body for other parents because it's necessary that they have a vote in this group. If that's the case, we need to hold an election where all of the Spanish-speaking parents recognize this group as representing them.]

These concerns about representation were shared by all parents at the initial meeting. Their desire to have all parents participate in the decision-making process to elect a representative body indicated that they saw themselves as part of the whole community, acting on behalf of others who shared similar interests and concerns. Although their intentions for democratic representation demonstrated a willingness by the parents to involve others, a problem arose when they attempted to call a meeting of all Spanish-speaking parents to vote on a representative group.

The original group of seven parents had been identified not only by Mr Ramos but also by School District personnel like Mr Clark, the Director of Special Projects, as consistently active in the schools. Because most of these parents had some experience with the schools and had expressed interest in participating in the parent leadership group, it seemed that the election might produce a cohort of people without as clear a vision of the purpose of the parent group. The parents, however, were intent on holding elections so that all Spanish-speaking parents could have a chance to participate in the decision-making group if they wished.

Before the meeting adjourned, as a researcher and facilitator, I presented a piece of information about the bilingual preschool advisory committee which met monthly with the preschool teacher. I shared data with them about the committee which I believed might be relevant to this group. The data included a description of the legal mandate which required that an advisory committee be established. The preschool advisory committee differed from the new group in that the preschool was mandated by federal law to have this committee whereas the new Spanish-speaking parent group emerged as a result of a need perceived by the parents involved. I described the structure of the advisory committee and the goals and logistics involved in conducting regular meetings. Mrs Hernandez immediately suggested that two parent representatives from this new group should go to observe the preschool advisory committee in action and report back to the new group. By the conclusion of this three-hour meeting the parents had discussed the need to endorse the concept of a parent leadership group and had reached agreement on holding elections for positions on the leadership body.

At the second meeting the initial group of seven parents attended and they welcomed ten others who had come to learn about the idea of this parent organization. Mrs Salinas, who had assumed uncontested leadership at the previous meeting, convened the meeting by suggesting that they begin without further delay. Everyone agreed and Mrs Salinas summarized what the group had accomplished at the first meeting. The information was received with overwhelming enthusiasm by all of the new parents present who testified, 'Ya era tiempo. Para mí es una idea fantástica porque muchos de nosotros necesitamos saber como navegarnos con la escuela y es necesario tener un grupo que nos apoye.' [It's about time. For me it's a fantastic idea because many of us need to know how to deal with the school and it's necessary to have a group like this to support us.]

A few parents raised questions about the role of this committee in relation to the other advisory committees for special projects like the bilingual preschool and the Migrant Education Program. A discussion ensued about the possible duplication of roles. One parent recalled that I had mentioned the difference between the mandated advisory committees and the new leadership group. I suggested that they could consider including representatives of the two other federally funded projects in their new parent organization so that they could become knowledgeable about the activities in the other groups, allowing for better coordination of activities. The parents accepted the suggestion and discussed the need to have representation of Spanish-speaking parents from all five schools.

Overall the meeting proved to be a great success. One parent summarized how necessary it was for parents to help each other and not just share problems. She explained:

Ya sabemos que unos de los problemas más grandes en la educación de nuestros niños es la mala comunicación entre los padres y los hijos, y entre los hijos y los maestros, pero el primer paso es ver que somos compañeros y aprender como ayudarnos. [We already know that one of the leading problems in our children's education is poor communication between parents and children and between our children and the teachers, but the first step is to see that we are colleagues and learn how to help each other.]

This basic premise was confirmed during the meeting as parents discussed the role they would play. One parent summarized this quite eloquently: 'Como dicen, yo vengo porque puedo no a ver si puedo.' [Like they say, I come because I can — not to see *if* I can.] While this loses some of its power in translation, its meaning reveals the confidence which some of the parents brought with them to the new organization and the spirit in which they cooperated with each other.

Mrs Salinas concluded the meeting by suggesting that the new group of parents who attended this meeting should be given the opportunity to participate in the leadership group if they wished. Others wanted to be sure that no one felt pressured. They circulated a piece of paper and parents signed their names and addresses if they were interested in committing themselves to working with the leadership group. One more parent signed up and the original group of seven became eight. Finally, one parent suggested that for the following meeting they should continue discussing their purpose and have parents report back on the visit to the preschool advisory committee meeting.

By doing they learned. Each time they met the parents understood that the task of organizing was meaningful because it meant a commitment to their children. Step by step parents learned the logistics of conducting meetings, as well as that listening to and respecting each other's points were necessary even when there was disagreement. They became more competent as they shared responsibility for obtaining the resources and information necessary to reach their goal. Visiting the preschool advisory committee meeting to learn how to conduct their own meetings is an example of this.

Motivation and Fear

At a subsequent meeting one of the parents who had visited the preschool was absent. The other parents who had attended regularly were present again, as were four of the officers of the preschool advisory committee. The meeting concentrated on how to organize their committee.

The parents visiting from the preschool advisory group asked the purpose of this committee. Mrs Salinas summarized it by saying that the group had begun meeting to see about organizing themselves to help their children succeed in school. Other parents added that they wanted as many parents as possible to work with them and to make the group function cooperatively. One person reported that at the previous meeting they had discussed the problem which many parents had in dealing with the school because notices were usually sent home in English and they missed out on a great deal of information. Mrs Salinas again reminded the parents that one of the most important functions of the group was to help one another, 'Como compañeros todos nos ayudamos.' [Like partners we all help one another.] One of the parents from the preschool advisory committee informed them that, 'A veces nosotros necesitamos presión para tomar responsabilidad. Somos Mexicanos y algo decidiosos y no debemos dejar que eso nos interrumpa este esfuerzo.' [Sometimes we need pressure to accept responsibility. We're Mexican and somewhat indecisive and we shouldn't let that interrupt our effort.] Another parent suggested that it was necessary to have more parents present to make a decision to organize. Mrs Salinas commented 'Pues esa es su opinión a ver que opinan otros.' [Well, that's your opinion, let's see what others think.] Another parent agreed that maybe it would be necessary to include more parents in case there were some who did not follow through with their commitment. Mrs Salinas argued, 'Pues, si tenemos padres poco incumplidos pero se tiene que comenzar en alguna parte.' [Some parents may be somewhat unreliable, but we have to start somewhere.] Most of the parents present agreed with the idea of forming the leadership group from those present.

Eleven parents arrived on time for the next meeting. All of the five schools were represented in this group. Although a room had been assigned to the parents' group, the door had not been opened. A student who was riding his bike around the school grounds reported that the school custodian had gone home ill. The parents decided to sit outside in some chairs that were stacked in the corner of the building, 'Asi estamos acostumbrados en el rancho,' [That's the way we do it the ranch,'] said one parent jokingly.

The meeting began outside and the group listened attentively to my data on the role of parents in Portillo schools. I reported on information I had collected about the lack of communication between Spanish-speaking parents in the schools. Some teachers believed that this meant that parents did not care about their children's learning because they measured 'caring' according to how well the children performed. That is, if children were high achievers, this was often attributed to how much parents helped them. If the children were underachieving and the parents did not make frequent contact with the school, they blamed the parents. If the children underachieved and the parents contacted the teachers for direction on how to help them at home, teachers believed that the children could achieve. One parent said,

> Nosotros les ayudamos a los niños en la casa con lo que sabemos, y muchas veces no es suficiente, pero tampoco las maestras nos dicen como es que les podemos ayudar. También ellas tienen que enseñar a los niños con buena voluntad. [We help our children at home as much as we can, and often it's not enough, but the teachers also do not tell us how to help our children. They also have to have good will in teaching our children.]

Although parents defended their efforts to assist, they also held the teachers responsible for their children's learning. One parent added, 'Muchos de nosotros trabajamos todo el día y nos cuesta dinero para salirnos del trabajo para ir hablar con los maestros. Así es que lo hacemos nomás cuando es de emergencia.' [Most of us work all day and we're docked in pay if we leave work to go to talk to the teachers. That's why we do it only in emergencies.] In essence, parents did not accept all the responsibility for their children's learning, nor did they agree with the teachers' perceptions about not caring about their children's learning if they failed to communicate with the school. Another parent explained how his desire to cooperate with the school was frustrating at times:

> A mí lo que me molesta es que me llamen al trabajo y me digan que mi hijo se está portando mal y luego pido permiso para salir y voy a la escuela y me hacen esperar una hora y luego salen a decirme que se han equivocado las secretarias y que no es mi hijo es otro muchacho que se está portando mal. Ya me ha pasado dos veces en la high school. [What upsets me is that the school calls me to tell me that my son has been misbehaving and I ask for permission to leave and I go to the school and they make me wait almost an hour and then they come out and tell me that they have made a mistake that it's someone else's kid that's been misbehaving. That's happened twice.]

There was a greal deal of discussion about the right of parents to appeal against the school's decision to discipline their children. This seemed to be an area where parents felt abused, as did the parent who was called about his son by mistake and made to wait while he lost pay. Others felt that it was unfair to have parents leave work and lose money when their children did not comply with the rules, especially because they believed that teachers were supposed to have control over the situation. The majority of these parents were unaware of parents' rights. The school had not made the rights known to them. Parents did not know that they could assert their rights to have the teacher deal fairly with their children.

Another issue raised by the parents was: '¿Cómo podemos comunicarnos con los maestros si trabajamos?' [How can we communicate with the schools if we work?] The response came from other parents who said that they found that calling the teacher sometimes worked and other times they sent notes to the teachers. Parents in the group had mixed experiences of the effectiveness of this strategy, depending on the type of problem at hand. Mrs Salinas insisted,

> Es importante que tengamos contacto con los maestros en persona porque hay muchas veces que los niños no tienen el problema y si los padres no investigan el problema, entonces los maestros siguen creyendo que el estudiante tiene la culpa. [It's important that we have personal contact with the teachers because often the child is not the problem and as long as we do not investigate the situation, the the teachers continue to think that the child is at fault.]

The parents concurred on the importance of making personal contact with the teacher whether the child was having problems or not. They recognized the need to communicate regularly with the schools about their children's progress as equally important.

Most parents had the impression that as long as the school did not contact them their children were doing fine. Thus they equated parent contact with problems — a concept familiar to most of them. These parents discovered the need to communicate regularly with the school in order to prevent problems and to insure the teachers that they did care and that their children had someone who supported them at home. As Mrs Hernandez commented, 'Parece que los maestros necesitan saber que nuestros hijos tienen a alguien que los apoya y que hable por ellos.' [It seems that teachers need to know that our children have someone who supports them and will speak on their behalf.] Certainly that had been the practice with many teachers. This pointed not only to the need for parents to understand how to communicate with the schools but also to the need for teachers to learn more about communicating with parents in order to make them real co-teachers.

The parents expressed interest in knowing about the School District's position on the organization of this group to represent Spanish-speaking families. The Director for Special Projects attended the latter part of this meeting and he addressed the parents in Spanish about the School District's view of parent involvement. Mr Clark complimented the parents on their commitment to help themselves and other parents to become involved in their children's education. He stated that across the state of California Mexican parents were becoming more active in the schools and that parents in this district had the potential to become one of the most effective organizations because this group organized voluntarily without federal mandate. Furthermore, the district superintendent endorsed Spanish-speaking parents becoming involved in the schools both financially and in policy. The Director of Special Projects urged the parents to take advantage of the supportive political climate in the District by organizing themselves in a formal group that could be recognized as a leadership body by the administration, the schools and the parents.

The parents listened attentively to Mr Clark's comments about the administration's support of Latino parent involvement. They asked him questions about meeting regularly with him or a District representative to discuss issues, '¿Con quién nos podemos reunir para discutir las necesidades de las familias? No es suficiente que nosotros aquí estemos hablando uno al otro sin que ustedes nos escuchen y nos apoyen. [Who can we meet with to discuss the need that our families have? It's not enough for us to talk to one another without having you listen to us and support us.] Mr Clark assured them that he planned to meet with them at least once a month and that it would also be important for them to have teachers from the different schools attend the meetings and present the teachers' perspective on programs for Spanish-speaking children. The parents agreed with this suggestion as a way to ascertain why teachers do what they do. One parent acknowledged, 'Es importante saber cómo piensan los maestros sobre los asuntos que nos urgen a nosotros. Posiblemente podemos invitar a maestros de cada escuela cada mes.' [It's important to know how teachers think about the issues that are important to us. Maybe we can invite the teachers from a different school each month.] Other parents agreed with the idea to meet with teachers.

The last issue discussed with Mr Clasrk was fiscal support of parent training, 'Nosotros necesitamos entrenamiento para padres que quieren aprender como ayudarles a sus hijos. ¿Tiene dinero el districto para ayudarnos?' [We need training for parents who want to learn how to help their children. Does the district have money to help us?] Mr Clark responded,

> Si, hay dinero para que vengan expertos en varias areas para padres y espero que la primera parte del año se dedique a un tema por ejemplo como ayudarle a los niños en matematicas y en la segunda parte del año en otro tema como lectura o alfabetismo. [Yes, there is money for experts to train the parents in various areas and I expect that the first part of the year will be devoted to one theme like training the parents to help their children in maths and the second part to another theme like literacy.]

The parents agreed with the possibility of training in these topics and cited personal experience in support of this proposal. They also commented on the need to organize a calendar to coordinate parent training because conflicting meetings detract from participation. Mr Clark said that he was looking into the possibility of hiring a part-time person to assist the parent group a few hours a month with logistics. The parents expressed the need for such a person especially since they had been forced to meet ouside even when they had officially requested a meeting room at the District office.

Parents' questions to the Director of Special Projects showed an interest in understanding the process of parental involvement and their role in leading the organization of Spanish-speaking parents. They recognized components of training such as the need to communicate with different levels of the educational system, assuring fiscal support, and coordination of meeting and training times to insure maximum participation by parents. Their comments indicated a desire to work cooperatively with the administration and the teachers to achieve more educational opportunities for Mexican students. Through collective endeavor, the parents' motivation helped them to persist beyond their fear.

Commitment

Commitment took on a special meaning for this group who again found themselves meeting outside in the parking lot when Mr Clark did not arrive. Parents spent the first half-hour trying to locate him and finally they called his home and found out that he was teaching a class that evening. The group decided that they should go ahead and meet in the parking lot since all eleven of them had made a commitment to arrive on time. One of the parents opened the meeting by admitting his fear of organizing other parents in the high school.

> Pues yo casi no he dormido esta semana desde que me dijeron que yo y mí compadre ibamos a tener que organizar a todos los padres de la escuela. Pues yo me imaginaba a mi y mi compadre pues como que llegamos pero no entramos. No sé como se sientan los demás. ¿No creen que sería posible que entre todos nos ayudaramos porque así acordamos?' [Well I've hardly slept this week since they told me that I had to organize the parents in the high school. Well I could imagine me and my compadre arriving at the school but not entering. I don't know how the others feel about it but wouldn't it be possible for us all to do it together since we said that we'd help each other?

Parents reminded him that they had decided to divide into teams, but revised the plan: 'Es cierto así nos apoyamos más. Entre todos podemos ir a cada escuela.'[That's true that way we can support each other more. We can all go to each school.] Parents agreed with the new plan to have the committee as a whole organize with each school.

The group then moved on to the strategy for organizing. They discussed the possibility of calling the parents from the school when they wanted to schedule a meeting. One parent, however, felt that the job should not be theirs alone and that the parents would respond to the invitation to meet if their committee was seen as legitimate by the principal's office. 'Primero vamos a la oficina y tenemos más apoyo si la oficina nos da el entre.' [First we'll go to the office and we'll have more support if the office sponsors us.] They agreed to have the committee deal directly with the principal in order to communicate with Spanish-speaking parents. One parent raised the concern that so many parents ignored invitations because they did not want to get involved. Mrs Solis then reminded the group, 'Nosotros somos responsables que ellos que no entiendan — que entiendan. Vamos enseñarles la importancia de que tomen responsabilidad por sus niños y ahora aquí nosotros comenzamos.' [We're responsible for making those parents who do not understand understand. We're going to show them the importance of taking responsibility for their children and here is where we begin.] The tone of the meeting changed and those parents who initially doubted their ability to deal with resistant or inactive parents nodded in agreement with this parent's appraisal of the situation and their role. Mr Solis further suggested, 'A ver cuáles son las cualidades que quieren en el presidente.'[Let's see what qualifications we want in the president.] Each person took a turn in describing the qualities they wanted in the president. The parents were sitting in a circle on the sidewalk in the school parking lot and one by one shared their perspectives.

Mrs H: Que tenga facilidad de palabra y que sea responsable, puntual. [Someone with good communication skills, responsible and punctual.]

Mr P: Que sea puntual. [To be punctual.]

Mr R: Responsable y que tenga iniciativa. [Someone responsible and with initiative.]

Mrs S: Expresiva y que sea responsable que nos ayude a apoyar, que no sea nomás en nombre. [Someone who is fluent and responsible and able to support us and not be (president) just in name.]

Mrs M: Que sepa poquito inglés. [Someone who knows a bit of English.]

Mrs R: Que tenga iniciativa sin que tengamos que empujarlo. [Someone who has initiative without having to be pushed.]

Mr B: Que pueda ayudarnos como lider. [Someone to help us like a leader.]

Mr M: Que nos ayuden a hablar con el personal de las escuelas. [To help us communicate with school personnel.]

Mr S: Yo creo que esa persona tiene que ayudarnos asemblar. [I think that peron should help us to assemble.]

Mr G: Que sepa organizar juntas y sea puntual. [Someone who knows how to organize meetings and to be punctual.]

The parents' comments indicate that they wanted a committed person who would assist them in organizing the group. Their view of commitment included keeping the rest of the parents enthusiastic about their responsibility. Despite the fact that the group had thus far operated in an egalitarian mode, the qualities they wanted in a president revealed the need for a strong leader. Prior to selecting the president, some parents had taken more initiative than others because they had more experience and saw what was needed to function as a group with a vision:

Mrs S: Me parece que es el propósito de este grupo es de concientizar a padres que sean padres que estén bien informados. La finalidad de nuestro comité es de ser un ejemplo noble para el pueblo. [I think that the purpose of this group is to make parents aware so that they become well informed. The main objective of our committee is to be a good example for our community.]

Mrs H: Eso es lo que vamos a tratar a hacer. [That's what we're going to try and do.]

Mr M: A veces nos sentimos poco, como es decir, sin sentirnos capacitados. [Sometimes we feel a bit like, I mean, like not able.]

Mr R: No nos sentimos capacitados por no tener escuela. [We don't feel able 'cause we don't have education.]

Mrs S: A veces decimos eso que no tenemos escuela pero la vida es una escuela pero tenemos experiencia y eso trabaja para nosotros. Necesitamos hacernos sentir que tenemos dirección. Ahora aquí estamos fijando una meta y es— ser gente comprometida. [Sometimes we use the fact that we haven't been to school as an excuse not to get involved, but we have experience and that works for us. We have to feel like we have a direction. Today we're here setting goals and being committed people.]

Mr P: Hasta para uno mismo—yo me sentía muy aislado antes y ahora en este grupo me han servido mucho estas juntas. [Even for me—I felt very isolated before and now in this group, these meetings have been very good for me.]

Mr R: Pierde uno la vergüenza. Con más confianza puede uno ir a las escuelas. [One loses one's shyness. We can visit the schools more confidently.]

Mr B: Pero siempre necesitamos alguien como presidente que sepa inglés. [But we still need someone as president who can speak English.]

Parents recognized that they had their own experience to share with others. They identified the most important goal of their group as the need to build consciousness among parents who feel isolated from the schools. The parents felt empowered by Mrs Solis' comments to them about their responsibility to use their life experience as part of their education. This raised the parents' awareness about their ability; previously they had believed a lack of schooling had limited them.

Mrs H: Pues, yo veo que la señora Solis que está bien preparada y podemos escoger a otra persona como secretaria. [Well, I see that Mrs Solis is well prepared and we can choose another person as a secretary.]

Mrs S: Pues yo sugeriria una pareja como los Hernandez. [Well I would suggest a couple like the Hernandez's.]

Mrs H: Y la Sra Salinas como secretaria. [And Mrs Salinas as secretary.]

Mrs S: Pues si porque yo he sido la secretaria para el programa migrante. [Well, yes because I've done it for the migrant program.]

Mr M: Pues si la Sra Solis está muy capacitada y puede elegir a otros que le ayuden. [Well, yes Mrs Solis is very able and qualified and she can elect others to help her.]
(Mrs Solis tried to tell them that she did not speak English and did not drive but the group would not accept that as an excuse. Mrs Salinas, the elected secretary, said that she would drive to meetings or other appointments when necessary.)

Election of leaders for the group took on an egalitarian character as parents proposed others for leadership positions and encountered general agreement. An interesting aspect was that parents did not vote on the leaders. It seemed that when a person was nominated, others joined in with supportive statements about the person named, but no vote was taken. When Mrs Solis suggested that a couple take the leadership, others did not acknowledge this recommendation because they recognized that she had excellent qualifications. They did not challenge Mrs Salinas' nomination because they understood that she had experience.

Once the parents had selected their leader they chose a name for the group. They wanted a name that reflected the composition of the group and could be referred to in an acronym. They decided to call themselves 'Comité de Padres Latinos — COPLA', which means couplet in Spanish.

Summary

The parents forged ahead as they talked about their concerns and in the process became convinced that they had the right, responsibility and power to deal with their children's academic and social concerns. However, they sometimes found the conditions for a meeting place less than ideal. They felt encouraged by the show of support from the District administration in accepting their organization and in the promise of assistance from a part-time aide to reserve a meeting room and to help them communicate with other parents.

An important feature of this process was parents' recognition that they had something to offer other parents. By sharing what they knew with other parents, they learned to become leaders and helped parents to realize that they were capable of making a difference in their children's education. As parents became more involved, they felt more in control of their situation. Feelings of incompetence create isolation for parents. Those feelings must be replaced with a recognition of the ability to collaborate with others before active participation can occur. That is, commitment to action is possible to the extent that parents feel worthy of contributing to others' learning. Parents also learned commitment in this process because, as a result of their participation, they became decision-makers.

The parents constructed a role for their group that reflected their desire to help parents become more aware of ways to cooperate with the schools and to help their children at home. Their perspective about parent involvement seemed consistent with their egalitarian mode of working with each other. They intended to work with the schools to make them more aware of Spanish-speaking families' needs, as well as to work with families to help them learn how to help their children and communicate with the schools. Their goals represented a model of participation that elevated the family to a position within the system that was worthy of acknowledgment and required accommodation within the school's curriculum. The School District's role as a supportive agent in the process was significant in that it represented commitment by the school to work with the families for the benefit of the students.

Chapter 9

Directions in Home and School Relationships

This study answered specific questions about the parents' role in their children's education and raised others pertaining to the home and school relationship. The study began by asking how these parents approached communication with their children at home and with the school in respect to children's literacy acquisition. I focused on parent–child interactions in the home, parent–teacher interactions in the school, and parent–parent interactions as they attempted to define their role in their children's education. These processes are endless and we needed to determine at what point we had answered the research question. It was established that the point at which to draw conclusions about the specific question was when parents had begun to accomplish the goals set out by the COPLA group to socialize each other about communication with their children and the schools. By the time I wrote the conclusion to this book the parent committee COPLA had organized satellite COPLA committees at the three elementary schools. Simultaneously they were planning to organize parents at the junior high and the high school. The model they devised extended to all Spanish-speaking parents in each school and to the teachers and the principal the invitation to communicate with them about their children's education. The response was successful in the initial meetings as Spanish-speaking parents in each school became convinced of the need to cooperate with the schools. The school principals also learned that the Spanish-speaking parents did not have to be isolated simply because they spoke only Spanish. The principals began a stronger effort to translate all notices to parents into Spanish and to involve some teachers to work directly with the COPLA group as liaison with other teachers in their respective schools. There was evidence of parents who had in a short time realized the value of collective work with other parents. They saw ways of acting when they confronted problems related to their children in school and they felt able to resolve problems that in the past would have persisted without any constructive solution.

For example, one parent in Maple School learned that her son had problems reading. She talked to one of the COPLA parents to obtain help. She was assisted first to contact the child's teacher and to inquire why the child might be doing poorly. When she spoke with the teacher, she learned that the teacher was insisting that the child should read in English because he seemed to talk to others in English. However, when he had read in English, he was unsuccessful. The parent told the teacher that her son had just begun to feel confident about speaking English and that she had learned in a parent meeting that it was not 'right' for children to be placed in English reading until they were fluent in English and could read well in their own language. The teacher agreed that maybe she was pushing him too fast into English reading. She stated that the child was not reading well in Spanish either. The parent then told the teacher that she could read to him at home in Spanish and she would help him as much as possible. Pleased at the parent's cooperative response, the teacher assured the parent that she would work with her son to raise his confidence about reading in Spanish before moving him to English.

This example illustrates the mother's internalization of skills for communicating with her child's teacher. Her request for assistance from the COPLA members helped her to reach the appropriate personnel to clarify the child's reading problem. The mother also used information from COPLA parent meetings at Maple School to understand her son's reading problem. This parent's ability to resolve her son's school problem represents the process of empowerment on three levels: first, for the parent who confidently applied her new knowledge; second, for the child through his mother's advocacy; and third, for the teacher who negotiated with the parent to benefit the student. In this example people were empowered by their ability to influence each other to affect the child's achievement, in establishing an avenue of communication that could facilitate mutual cooperation.

A different example of empowerment was cited by one parent who had been active with the COPLA group since its inception. This parent stated that his son was only in kindergarten, but he was curious about the frequent night parent meetings that his father attended. His son's questions about the meeting provided him with ample opportunity to communicate with his son about school. The parent said that in the past he would not have understood the need to talk to children about the things that go on in school meetings, but since his involvement with COPLA, he realized the importance of communicating with his child about the meetings. He wanted his son to know that he cared to learn about the school by becoming involved in COPLA. The father's relationship with COPLA opened up a new reason for communication within the family. These changes in the home setting signalled a new consciousness about the nature of parent–child communication on the part of the father. Through collective organization with other parents this father empowered himself and his child.

The Portillo study yielded the following major findings.

1 Literacy activities in the home and school revealed the systematic patterning of relationships within the family and between the family and the schools. The arrangements observed through interaction provide a view of sociocultural coherence, i.e. language, values, resources, cultural knowledge and meaning, which are the undergirding motivators for families' roles in their children's education.

2 Mexican parents cared about their children's education but often lacked the necessary skills to participate as the school required.

3 The parents' involvement in their organization made their participation more meaningful. Their ability to transcend communication barriers with the school by determining their own goals and discovering their meaning in the process constituted empowerment.

4 A more hypothetical point deals with the lack of communication found between the Spanish-speaking parents and the school. This isolation occurred for many, in spite of the fact that some teachers and other school personnel were bilingual. This implies that language is only part of the problem. It could be hypothesized that English-speaking parents also experience isolation and frustration in dealing with the school. Their ability to speak the 'correct' language does not guarantee knowledge of how to deal with school culture.

Parent Involvement in Literacy

The role of parent involvement in literacy for the Spanish-speaking group in Portillo makes sense only when we understand the historical dynamics of the community and its people. Portillo has seen many changes in social and political climate which have given rise to educational opportunities for English- and Spanish-speaking groups. Early segregated schools in the 1940s and tracking in schools in the 1950s limited educational attainment and participation for Mexicans in Portillo. Through the efforts of long-time community residents and leadership in the Mexican community, educational programs that targeted the Spanish-speaking students' academic standing came to fruition. Special attention to the needs of Spanish-speaking children became a priority with the establishment of the bilingual program, the Migrant Program, the bilingual preschool and Project Vision. Leaders of these programs became strong advocates for Mexican children and their families with respect to schooling.

This study viewed parent involvement as a critical component in children's overall literacy acquisition, as well as in their success in school. Parents as well as teachers played an active role in children's learning. Both the home and the school shared the responsibility for children's learning, and the home emerged as a vital part of children's literacy development as a result of diverse parent-child interactions around non-school-related literacy activities. In terms of school-related activities parents played a major role in homework preparation and school communication, essential aspects of children's success in school.

Regarding parents and the school, parents valued schooling and were concerned about their children's schooling. They demonstrated this in numerous ways including providing children with nurturing learning environments at home filled with conversation about family events, discussion of daily routines, reading of favorite storybooks to children, helping children organize their homework settings and often assisting them in completing homework assignments.

Parents participated in their children's schooling at different levels. Some only helped the children with school work, others communicated with the schools, and others participated in training workshops and governance; what they did depended on their level of acculturation into the school system. The degree to which parents internalize new values and practices of communication with their children determines the changes that occur at home. As new practices such as helping children to complete their homework begin in the home, they also affect the school setting. For example, the way that parents initiate communication with teachers is illustrated by the report at the beginning of this chapter of the way a mother handled her son's reading problem. Regardless of the degree of acculturation or the student's level of achievement in school, Mexican parents valued education for their children. This interest was constrained only by the lack of systematic training for parents and of involvement in the schools. This lack of communication between the school and the home caused many Spanish-speaking parents to feel isolated and ignorant about their role in their children's schooling. Parents also felt isolated because they spoke Spanish while most activities in the schools occurred in English. They had to learn that the notion of participating in schooling requires a series of sociocultural skills including knowing when to contact the school, knowing whom to contact, and knowing how to address school personnel to support one's rights.

Role of Advocates

While all families cared about their children's schooling, few knew what the school expected from them. They lacked knowledge and experience to deal with the school. This indicates the value of the preschool experience for Spanish-speaking students because the teacher spoke Spanish and knew the families and community. She reached out to parents in a way that enabled them to participate in Spanish and to feel able to teach their children. Parents were encouraged to use family events and their own language to talk and read about things the children liked. They were also taught to be informed consumers of educational programs and materials which could be instructive to the children. While this may be interpreted as another form of imposing the school's agenda on the family's, thus promoting the deficit theory, the approach in Portillo differed in three important ways: (1) the preschool teacher used the family's activities and taught them to be more conscious of their own interactions with their children; (2) she organized a parent committee which involved parents in the decision-making activities of the preschool; (3) she incorporated the students' culture into the daily school curriculum and instruction. Thus the preschool experience represented a culturally congruent educational experience. The preschool teacher's role was that of an advocate, which was a key role also played by other Portillo personnel in relating to the Spanish-speaking community.

Spanish-speaking parents needed school personnel to reach out to them in their own language and to speak for them on issues of their children's achievement in the classroom, their role in school-related activities in the home and their ability to guide their children through school at different levels. Advocates provided the school part of the equation in an effective parent education model. Behaviors which most characterized the advocates for Spanish-speaking families, like the preschool teacher and other school district personnel, included their ability to speak the parents' language, their readiness to give parents a decision-making role in special programs, and their ability to motivate Spanish-speaking parents to participate in special workshops.

A consequence of the cumulative efforts of parental involvement projects was the COPLA, which helped to reverse the unidirectional communication between home and school. As parents participated actively in the development of goals for learning to interact in their children's schooling, they empowered themselves, their children and the teacher.

The Convergence of Theory and Method

These findings suggest that the deficit perspective is an invalid explanation of why Mexican parents do not help their children in school. Application of the cultural deficit hypothesis would locate the problem of home-school communication in Spanish-speaking families' homes and would consider the language and cultural differences as genetic problems rather than differences to be reckoned with by the school based on the premise of inequity. The deficit perspective also recognizes the unrelenting power of the school as the sole authority in the education process in requiring total rejection of linguistic and cultural differences and demanding assimilation to the new culture. This study negates the cultural deficit notion by revealing the influence of sociocultural factors in the daily interactions between parents and children, parents and teachers, and parents and parents.

The ability of parents to go beyond their perceived limitations to influence structural change makes the concept of empowerment a theoretical explanation which merits consideration. The theoretical premise for the study of literacy in the home and school, while examining the role of parental involvement in the process, is integrally related to the methods used in this study. As I designed the study of literacy practices in the school and the home, I began with the theoretical premise that literacy is a socially constituted activity which requires a stimulating interactive learning environment in the home and the school. Following this assumption, family literacy activities, as well as those in the school, had to be examined. Ethnographic strategies produced data on the sociocultural features of the activities and revealed the social meanings that were internalized by individuals involved in interaction. The social meaning which words held for the children, parents and teachers could be considered the thread by which this community weaves itself into one cloth.

Ethnographic studies have contributed a great deal to the examination of linguistic minorities and education. In compliance with the axioms in ethnographic research, I remained open to follow the process of interaction around literacy as it developed in the home and the school. As I probed deeper in search of a holistic perspective on the role of the home and school in literacy learning, the issue of parent involvement overlaid the literacy activities and ultimately the children's literacy achievement in school.

The parents and school personnel played an active role in analyzing the data which gave rise to the development of a parent organization, COPLA. This feature of the study contributed to parents' awareness of their perceived condition of social isolation and encouraged them to organize a parent leadership group. The researcher's role in facilitating this group was a form of intervention designed with three specific purposes in mind: first, to share the research findings with parents in a way that would inform them and develop their organization by helping the Spanish-speaking families to understand the nature of their role in their children's education; second, to study further the acculturation process of these families as they became socialized to cooperate with the school; and third, to have the parents assume leadership of their group and to determine their own meaning and goals for their role in their children's education. This process of facilitating parent organization represents an expansion of the researcher's role in an educational ethnographic study. In a heuristic way this expanded role constitutes a theoretical development in research involving applied ethnography in an educational setting. This study has demonstrated the possibility of conducting scientific and systematic research while utilizing the flexibility of the methodology to intervene for the purpose of empowering the participants and studying the intervention. Society has a legitimate role to play in the functioning of American families, and this study of applied ethnography represents a model for accommodating theory, methodology and intervention in achieving effective family-school relationships.

Empowerment: A Hypothesis

As a result of the convergence of theory and method, parents became empowered. This took many forms. Occasional parent workshops were held by individual schools and special programs such as the Migrant Education Program. The objective was to raise parent awareness on specific topics. Through a series of sessions during the year parents learned how to discipline their children at home and how to talk with them about their school and other issues. These workshops followed a family influence model in that they were designed to change family practices to conform to those of the school. Other workshops held by programs such as Migrant Education could also be construed along the lines of the family influence model, except that they had a purpose beyond that of making parents' behavior congruent with that of schools. This was to give parents some decision-making power to organize their parent education program. In this case the presentations made to parents by local community agencies on AIDS, drugs, immigration, and child abuse in the home contributed to parents' overall awareness about their role in their children's education. The parents learned about community agencies that could assist them with social, medical and legal needs in the family. The question, however, remained as to how the school, with the exception of the preschool program, used knowledge about the families to diversify the curriculum and instruction best to serve the students. The extent to which the school expected only the family to accommodate to the school's expectations assumes that the family unit was deficient in knowledge about educating the child and participating in the school. Furthermore, parents were expected to conform to standards operative in the school. Although each aspect of the parent involvement effort for Spanish-speaking families in and of itself did not constitute a comprehensive plan for helping parents participate meaningfully in their children's education, the cumulative effect was to contribute to the parents' general knowledge and to lay the foundation for them to organize their own decision-making group to socialize each other.

The parents' effort to affect school policies and practices and to get educators to deal with them more effectively produced change in a two-way direction. The parents intended to have the schools pay attention to their needs on matters of sending home communications in Spanish, and they also intended to reach out to other Spanish-speaking families to encourage them to communicate more frequently with the school. Holding both the school and the families responsible for the children's academic success constitutes a cooperative systems model in that parents had as their goal the encouragement of dialogue and negotiation in resolving their children's educational problems.

Three models for parent involvement were described in Chapter 3: how the school attempts to influence the family; how the parents attempt reform; and how the school and the home form a cooperative systems model. These depict outcomes of the relationship between families and schools. The family influence model and the school reform model are inherently limited in relation to empowerment outcomes. The cooperative systems model closely resembles the findings in this study. That is, when the school respected and incorporated the family's culture as part of the education system and when the parents had decision-making power and learned how to negotiate with the school for their children's needs, all parties involved become empowered. Parents were capable of socializing each other and learned how to help their children in the home as well as becoming involved with the schools. Furthermore, parents learned that skills and procedures to help their children were acquired abilities. This dispelled the isolation of powerlessness. Their role as advocates for Spanish-speaking students played a significant part in helping parents learn how to help their children. The district parent organization, COPLA, was a result of the cumulative effect of the various parent involvement efforts that spoke on behalf of parents, such as the Migrant Education parent meetings, training workshops and the preschool parent training sessions. However, only the preschool program represented a comprehensive model for maximizing home-school cooperation for children's achievement which had positive effects as long as four years afterwards, as this study shows with the performance of the advanced readers. How parents learn to become their own leaders and advocates for other parents became a critical part of the study. We noted that as Spanish-speaking parents learned more about the schools and their rights and responsibilities regarding their children's schooling, they assumed a leadership role in organizing other members of their community for the purpose of collectively learning how to help their children by cooperating with the schools. This process empowered them and influenced structural change.

Implications for Practice and Policy

The parent organization program which was initiated by the parents and the researcher combined three strategies: (1) application of a theoretical and empirical knowledge base; (2) participation of parents in decision-making and design of goals related to their needs for information and skills regarding their parenting functions; and (3) integration of programs that included family contact with schools and other agencies in the community. Schools considering the development of a parent involvement program need to consider these three facets.

Policy implications exist for different levels of the school's relationship with Spanish-speaking families: the school level, the District level and the state level. At the school level the District policies need to address the practice of communicating with parents in Spanish, making translation services available at meetings, providing appropriate and systematic training about the operation of the school and ways to help children in the home. Most importantly, the teachers need to be supported with incentives to work with parents. At the broader District level administrative policy needs to reflect the cooperative spirit which solicits Spanish-speakers' participation in decision-making and provides teachers with training and evaluation of their skills in working with parents. At the state level policy needs to mandate training for teachers to provide education to parents. The California State Department of Education and the University of California have jointly promoted research in the area of training teachers to work with parents.

Directions for Research

What do we really need to know about parent education? We need to know more about the theoretical basis on which we conduct research on parent education, particularly as it affects minority communities (Laosa, 1983). While much parent education research has focused on how to influence and reform home childrearing practices for the child's academic success, more needs to be known about the way that the school views the family. In providing systematic opportunities for parents to learn more about the school, what do we know about the family and how can the school learn more about family activities to help diversify school activities? We need to expand the school's role in learning about families and working with parents to understand how children learn at home. Hypothetically, if the ideal model is a two-way street of communication between school and home, then this is the part of the street that Portillo has yet to develop. With the exception of the preschool, the remaining grades need to develop a systematic way of communicating with families and learning how to provide the best program by learning about home activities.

Parent education in any form may provide a valuable service to children, to the school and the family as a whole, as noted in many studies. The potential danger of dealing with the issue of parent education lies in our tendency to consider parent education as a family influence issue to make the family conform to the school. This becomes a problem if we neglect to deal with the role of the school in making changes to deal with students' special needs. Another aspect of parent education for Spanish-speaking families is that we are often led to believe that providing parents with training helps to integrate them into the mainstream of the school system. Thus, in the name of equity, parents are provided with special training to help them and their children fit into the system. Part of the process of integrating minority families into the school system involves a cultural change on the part of the families. Therefore, if the families do not participate in their own process of change, they do not internalize the change nor are they actually participants in the system. They are merely seen as objects of the schools' needs.

We cannot deny that minority families must have every opportunity to participate in the school system. However, participation in the system constitutes an opportunity not just to be affected by the system but also to affect it. Without this balance parent participation becomes merely an aspect of hegemony on the part of the school.

The tension between the deficit model and equity can best be resolved through research that focuses on the nature of the parent education program in the context of a particular community. The Portillo study attempted to address the changes that immigrant families experienced in adapting to a new society in which they had not been educated. The parents' efforts to organize themselves in COPLA constituted a realization on the part of both the schools and the parents that they needed a change to benefit the children's schooling.

The Portillo study provided a window through which I could examine parent participation through family and school literacy practices and a door through which I, as a researcher, could step to help to facilitate parents' organization and involvement. Overall, the study showed that the school expected Spanish-speaking parents to participate in the schools. Communication with the schools requires specific sociocultural knowledge implicit in behaviors and language. However, learning new language and behaviors did not constitute cultural change for the parents until they were able to create their own meaning by joining collectively to construct knowledge and awareness about their role in their children's education — a role which COPLA, as a structure for participation, helped to shape. As parents interacted more with the schools, the schools were also forced to change to accommodate the participation of Spanish-speaking parents by using their language.

The final chapter is yet to be written. While we were able to establish the sociocultural nature of parental involvement relative to literacy, the cultural transmission aspect of the process remains to be studied. We need to know how the COPLA leadership group will execute their newly assumed responsibility and how effective they will be in motivating parents and educators to work together. How will these parents who assumed leadership transmit the knowledge to other Spanish-speaking parents as they socialize others into the school culture? The other question to be examined is how the School District responds to parents' efforts to involve themselves in the schools. Finally, how will the new practices affect school and District policy on parent participation? As these questions are answered through research, the families and the schools will have a stronger basis for communicating with each other and literacy can be better understood in relation to the home-school communication that unquestionably empowers all those involved in the process.

Bibliography

ALBERT, R. S. and RUNCO M. A. (1985) 'Personality and family variables and exceptionally gifted boys' creative potential.' Paper presented at the Conference of the American Psychological Association, Los Angeles, CA, August.

AU, K. H. (1979) 'Using the experience-text-relationship method with minority children.' *The Reading Teacher,* 32, 677–9.

AU, K. H. (1980) 'Participation structures in a reading lesson with Hawaiian children: Analysis of a culturally appropriate instructional event.' *Anthropology and Education Quarterly,* 11, 91–115.

AU, K. H. and JORDAN, C. (1981) 'Teaching reading to Hawaiian children: Finding a culturally appropriate solution.' In H. T. TRUEBA, G. P. GUTHRIE and K. H. AU (Eds). *Culture in the Bilingual Classroom: Studies in Classroom Ethnography* (pp. 139–152). Rowley, MA: Newbury House.

AU, K. H. and KAWAKAMI, A. J. (1982) 'A conceptual framework for studying the long-term effects of comprehension instruction.' *The Quarterly Newsletter of the Laboratory of Comparative Human Cognition,* 6, 95–100.

AU, K. and KAWAKAMI, A. (1984) 'Vygotskian perspective on discussion process in small-group reading lessons.' In P. L. PETERSON, L. C. WILKINSON and M. HALLINAN (Ed.,), *The Social Context of Instruction: Group Organization and Group Processes* (pp. 209–25). New York: Academic Press.

BARR, D., COCHRAN, M., RILEY, D. and WHITMAN, M. (1984) 'Family empowerment: An interview.' *Human Ecology Forum,* 14, 4–13.

BECHER, R. M. (1984) 'Parent Involvement: A review of research and principles of successful practice.' National Institute of Education, Washington, DC.

BEREITER, C. and ENGLEMAN, S. (1966) *Teaching Disadvantaged Children in Preschool.* Englewood Cliffs, NJ: Prentice-Hall.

BERGER, P. and NEUHAUS, R. (1977) *To Empower People: The Role of Mediating Structures in Public Policy.* Washington, DC: American Enterprise Institute for Public Policy Research.

BLOOM, B. S. (1981) *All Our Children Learning.* New York: McGraw-Hill.

BLOOM, B. S. (1985) *Developing Talent in Young People.* New York: Ballantine Books.

BLOOME, D. (Ed.) (1987) Literacy and Schooling. Norwood, NJ: Ablex.

BOULDER VALLEY, Colorado School District, (1975) *A Personalized Kindergarten Program with Supplementary Parent Involvement.* Final Report Submitted to the Bureau of Elementary and Secondary Education, Washington, DC: Office of Education.

BRONFENBRENNER, U. (1974a) *A Report on Longitudinal Evaluations of Preschool Programs, Vol. 2: Is Early Intervention Effective?* Washington, DC: Office of Child Development.

BRONFENBRENNER, U. (1974b) 'The origins of alienation.' *Scientific American,* 231, 53–61.

BRONFENBRENNER, U. (1979a) *The Ecology of Human Development: Experiments by Nature and Design.* Cambridge, MA: Harvard University Press.

BRONFENBRENNER, U. (1979b) 'Beyond the deficit model in child and family policy.' *Teacher's College Record,* 81, 95–104.

BROWN, G. H., ROSEN, N. L., HILL, S. T. and OLIVAS, M. A. (1980) *The Condition of Education for Hispanic Americans.* Washington, DC: US Government Printing Office.

CALDWELL, J. (1979) *Carpinteria as It Was.:* Papillon Press.

CAMPOS, J. and KEATINGE, R. (1984) *The Carpinteria Preschool Program: Title VII Second Year Evaluation Report.* Washington, DC: Department of Education.

CAMPOS, J and KEATINGE, R. H. (1987) *Project Vision: A Program for Potentially Gifted LEP-Hispanic Children.* Report submitted to Washington, DC, Office of Bilingual Education.

CAMPOS, S. and KEATINGE, R. (1988) 'The Carpinteria Language Minority student experience from theory to practice to success.' In T. SKUTNABD-KANGAS and J. CUMMINS (Eds), *Minority Education* (pp. 299–307). Clevedon, Avon, England: Multilingual Matters Ltd.

CHILCOTT, J. H. (1987) 'Where are you coming from and where are you going? The reporting of ethnographic research.' *American Educational Research Journal,* 24, 199–218.

CLARK, R. M. (1983) *Family Life and School Achievement: Why Poor Black Children Succeed or Fail.* Chicago IL: University of Chicago Press.

CLARK, M. (1984) 'Literacy at home and at school: Insights from a study of young fluent readers.' In H. GOELMAN, A. OBERG and F. SMITH (Eds), *Awakening to Literacy* (pp. 38–50). Portsmouth, NH: Heinemann.

COCHRAN, M. (1987) 'The parental empowerment process: Building on family strengths.' *Equity and Choice,* 4, 9–23.

COCHRAN, M. and HENDERSON, C. R., Jr. (1986) 'Family matters: Evaluation of the parental empowerment program.' Unpublished paper. Ithaca, NY: Cornell University.

COCHRAN, M. and WOOLEVER, F. (1983) 'Beyond the deficit model: The empowerment of parents with information and informal supports.' In I. E. SIEGEL and L. P. LAOSA (Eds), *Changing Families* (pp. 225–45). New York: Plenum.

COLE, M. (1981) *The Zone of Proximal Development: Where Culture and Cognition Create Each Other.* Report No. 106. San Diego, CA: University of California, Center for Human Information Processing.

COLE, M. (1985) 'The zone of proximal development: Where culture and cognition create each other.' In J. V. WERTSCH (Ed.), *Culture, Communication, and Cognition: Vygotskian Perspectives* (pp. 146–61). Cambridge, MA: Cambridge University Press.

COLE, M. and D'ANDRADE, R. (1982) 'The influence of schooling on concept formation: Some preliminary conclusions.' *The Quarterly Newsletter of the Laboratory of Comparative Human Cognition,* 4, 19–126.

COLE, M. and GRIFFIN, P. (1983) 'A socio-historical approach to re-mediation.' *The Quarterly Newsletter of the Laboratory of Comparative Human Cognition,* 5, 69–74.

COLE, M., GAY, J., GLICK, J. A. and SHARP, D. (1971) *The Cultural Context of Learning and Thinking.* New York: Basic Books.

COLEMAN, J. S. (1966) *Equality of Educational Opportunity Submitted to the US Department of Health, Education and Welfare.* Washington, DC:US Government Printing Office.

COLEMAN, J. S. (1987) 'Families and schools.' *Educational Researchers,* 16, 6, 32–8,

COMER, J. P. (1984) 'Home-school relationships as they affect the academic success of children.' *Education and Urban society,* 16, 323–37.

COOK-GUMPERZ, J. (1986) *The Social Construction of Literacy.* Cambridge: Cambridge University Press.

CORTEZ, C. (1986) 'The education of language minority students: A contextual interaction model.' In *Beyond Language: Social and Cultural Factors in Schooling Language Minority Students* (pp. 3–34). Los Angeles, CA: California State University, Evaluation, Dissemination and Assessment Center.

COSER, R. L. (1967) *Life-cycle and Achievement in America.* New York: Harper and Row.

CREMIN, L. A. (1976) *Public Education.* New York: Basic Books.

CREMIN, L. A. (1977) *Traditions of American Education.* New York: Basic Books.

CUMMINS, J. (1986) 'Empowering minority students: A framework for intervention.' *Harvard Educational Review,* 56, 18–36.

DE AVILA, E. (1986) 'Motivation, intelligence, and access: A theoretical framework for the education of minority language students.' *Issues in English Language Development* (pp. 121–31). Washington DC: National Clearinghouse for Bilingual Education.

DE CASTELL, S., LUKE, A. and EGAN, K. (Eds) (1986) *Literacy, Society, and Schooling.* New York: Cambridge University Press.

DELGADO-GAITAN, C. (1987a) 'Compassion and concern: Mentoring students through high school.' *Urban Education,* 8, 93–102.

DELGADO-GAITAN, C. (1987b) 'The traditions and transitions in the learning process of Mexican children: An ethnographic view.' In G. and L. SPINDLER (Eds), *Interpretive Ethnography of Education* (pp. 333–62). Hillsdale, NJ: Lawrence Erlbaum.

DELGADO-GAITAN, C. (1987c) 'Mexican adult literacy: New directions for immigrants.' In S. GOLDMAN and H. TRUEBA (Eds), *Becoming Literate in English as a Second Language: Advances in Research and Theory* (pp. 9–32). Norwood, NJ: Ablex.

DELGADO-GAITAN, C. (1988) 'The value of conformity: Learning to stay in school.' *Anthropology and Education Quarterly,* 19, 2, 354–82.

DELGADO-GAITAN, C. (1989a) 'Classroom literacy activity for Spanish-speaking students.' *Linguistics in Education,* 1, 3, pp. 285–97.

DELGADO-GAITAN, C. (1989b) 'Socializing children to school culture.' Unpublished manuscript. University of California, Santa Barbara.

DEUTSCH, M. (Ed.) (1967) *The Disadvantaged Child.* New York: Basic Books.

DIAZ, S., MOLL, L. and MEHAN, H. (1986) 'Sociocultural resources in instruction: A context specific approach.' In *Beyond Language: Social and Cultural Factors in Schooling Language Minority Students* (pp. 187–238). Los Angeles, CA: California State University, Evaluation, Dissemination and Assessment Center.

DUNN, L. (1987) *Bilingual Hispanic Children on the US Mainland: A Review of Research on Their Cognitive, Linguistic and Scholastic Development*. Research Monograph. American Guidance Service. Minnesota Circle Pines.

DURAN, R. (1983) 'Cognitive theory in Chicano children's oral reading behavior.' *Quarterly Newsletter of the Laboratory of Human Cognition*, 5, 23–5.

EPSTEIN, J. L. (1987) 'Effects on student achievement of teachers' practices of parental involvement.' In S. SILVERN (Ed.) *Literacy through Family Community and School Interactions* (pp. 98–110). Greenwich, CT: JAI.

ERICKSON, F. (1984) 'School literacy, reasoning, and civility: An anthropologist's perspective.' *Review of Educational Research*, 54, 525–44.

ERICKSON, F. and SCHULTZ, J. J. (1977) 'When is a context? Some issues and methods in the analysis of social competence.' *The Quarterly Newsletter of the Institute for Comparative Human Development*, 1, 5–10.

FLAVELL, J. H., SPEER, J. R., GREEN, F. L. and AUGUST, D. L. (1981) *The Development of Comprehension Monitoring and Knowledge abut Communication*. Monograph of the Society for Research in Child Development, 46.

FREIRE, P. (1970) *Pedagogy of the Oppressed*. New York: Continuum.

FREIRE, P. (1973) *Education for Critical Consciousness*. New York: Continuum.

FREIRE, P. (1985) *The Politics of Education*. South Hadley, MA: Bergin and Garvey.

FREIRE, P. and MACEDO, D. (1987) *Literacy: Reading the Word and the World*. South Hadley, MA: Bergin and Garvey.

GARCIA, P. and MALDONADO, L. A. (1982) 'America's Mexican: A plea for specificity.' *Social Science Journal*, 19, 9–24.

GEERTZ, C. (1973) 'Thick description.' In *Interpreting culture* (pp. 3–32). New York: Basic Books.

GILMORE, P. (1983) 'Spelling Mississippi: Recontextualizing a literacy related speech event.' *Anthropology and Educational Quarterly*, 14, Winter, 235–55.

GOELMAN, H., OBERG, A. and SMITH, F. (Eds) (1984) *Awakening to Literacy*. Portsmouth, NH: Heinemann Educational Books.

GOLDENBERG, C. N. (1987) 'Low-income Hispanic parents' contributions to their first-grade children's word-recognition skills.' *Anthropology and Education Quarterly*, 18, 149–79.

GOODSON, B. D. and HESS, R. (1975) *Parents as Teachers of Young Children: An Evaluative Review of Some Contemporary Concepts and Programs*. Washington, DC: Bureau of Educational Personnel Development, DHEW, Office of Education.

GORDON, I. (1978) 'What does research say about the effects of parent involvement on schooling?' Paper presented at the Annual Meeting of the Association for Supervision and Curriculum Development. Chicago, IL.

GOTTS, E. E. (1980) 'Long-term effects of a home-oriented preschool program.' *Childhood Education*, 56, 228–34.

GRIFFITHS, A. and HAMILTON, D. (1984) *Parent, Teacher and Child: Working together in Children's Learning*. London: Heinemann Educational Books.

GRIFFORE, R. and BOGER, R. (Ed.) (1986) *Child Rearing in the Home and School*. New York: Plenum.

GROSS, M. J., RIDGLEY, E. M. and GROSS, A. E. (1974) *Combined Human Efforts in Elevating Achievement at the Wheatley School.* Washington, DC (ERIC Document Reproduction Service No. ED 102 666).

GUMPERZ, J. (1971) *Language in Social Groups.* Palo Alto, CA: Stanford University Press.

GUMPERZ, J. (1986) 'Interactional sociolinguistics in the study of schooling.' In J. COOK-GUMPERZ (Ed.), *The Social Construction of Literacy* (pp. 45–68). Cambridge, MA: Cambridge University Press.

HAKUTA, K. S. and DIAZ, R. M. (1985) 'The relationship between degree of bilingualism and cognitive ability: A critical discussion and new longitudinal data.' In K. E. NELSON (Ed.), *Children's Language* (Vol. 5, pp. 319–45). Hillsdale, NJ: Erlbaum.

HEATH, S. B. (1982a) 'Questioning at home and at school: A comparative study.' In G. SPINDLER (Ed.), *Doing the Ethnography of Schooling* (pp. 102–30). New York: Holt Rinehart and Winston.

HEATH, S. B. (1982b) 'What no bedtime story means: Narrative skills at home and school.' *Language in Society,* 11, 49–76.

HEATH, S. B. (1983) *Ways with Words.* Cambridge: Cambridge University Press.

HERMAN, J. L. and YEH, J. P. (1980) *Some Effects of Parent Involvement in Schools.* Los Angeles, CA: Center for the Study of Evaluation.

HESS, R. D. and SHIPMAN, V. C. (1965) 'Early experience and the socialization of cognitive modes in children.' *Child Development,* 36, 869–85.

HOFFMAN, L. W. (1974) 'Effects of maternal employment on the child: Review of the research.' *Developmental Psychology,* 10, 204–28.

HOLTZMAN, W., DIAZ-GUERRERO, R. and SWARTZ, J. (1975) *Personality Development in Two Cultures: A Cross-cultural Longitudinal Study of School Children in Mexico and the United States.* Austin, TX: University of Texas Press.

HOWARD, A. (1974) *Ain't No Big Thing: Coping Strategies in a Hawaiian-American Community.* Honolulu: The University of Hawaii Press.

IRVINE, D. J. (1979) *Parent Involvement Affects Children's Cognitive Growth.* Albany, NY: University of the State of New York, State Education Department, Division of Research.

JORDAN, C. (1984) 'Cultural compatibility and the education of ethnic minority children.' *Educational Research Quarterly,* 8, 59–71.

KARRAKER, R. J. (1972) 'Increasing academic performance through home-managed contingency programs.' *Journal of School Psychology,* 10, 173–9.

LAMB, M. (Ed) (1976) *The Role of Father in Child Development.* New York: Wiley.

LAOSA, L. M. (1977) 'Maternal teaching strategies in Mexican American families: factors affecting intra-group variability in how mothers teach their children.' Paper presented at the Annual Meeting of the American Educational Research Association, New York, April.

LAOSA, L. M. (1978) 'Maternal teachings strategies in Chicano families of varied educational and socioeconomic levels.' *Child Development,* 49, 1129–35.

LAOSA, L. M. (1982) 'School, occupation, culture, and family: The impact of parental schooling on the parent-child relationship.' *Journal of Educational Psychology,* 74, 791–827.

LAOSA, L. M. (1983) 'Parent education, cultural pluralism, and public policy: The uncertain connection.' In R. HASKINS and D. ADAMS (Eds), *Parent Education and Public Policy* (pp. 331–45). Norwood, NJ: Ablex.

LAREAU, A. (1987) 'Social class differences in family-school relationships: The importance of cultural capital.' *Sociology of Education*, 60, 73–85.

LAZAR, I. and DARLINGTON, R. B. (1978) *Summary: Lasting Effects after Preschool.* Monograph Series Paper. Consortium for Longitudinal Studies. New York: Cornell University.

LEICHTER, H. J. (1974) 'Some perspectives on the family as educator.' In H. J. LEICHTER (Ed), *The Family as Educator* (pp. 86–101). New York: Teachers College Press.

LEICHTER, H. J. (1979) 'Families and communities as educators: Some concepts of relationships.' In H. J. LEICHTER (Ed), *Families and Communities as Educators* (pp. 11–23). New York: Teachers College Press.

LEICHTER, H. J. (1984) 'Families as environments for literacy.' In H. GOELMAN, A. OBERG and F. SMITH (Eds), *Awakening to Literacy* (pp. 38–50). Portsmouth, NH: Heinemann Educational Books.

LELER, H. (1983) 'Parent education and involvement in relation to the schools and to parents of school-aged children.' In R. HASKINS and D. ADAMS (Eds), *Parent Education and Public Policy*, (pp. 149–61). Norwood, NJ: Ablex.

LEVINE, R. and WHITE, M. (1986) *Human Conditions: The Cultural Basis of Educational Developments.* New York: Routledge and Kegan Paul.

MCCONNELL, B. (1976) *Bilingual Mini-school Tutoring Project. A State of Washington URRD (Urban, Rural, Racial, Disadvantaged) Program.* (ERIC Reproduction Service No. Ed 135 508).

MCCONNELL, B. (1979) *Individualized Bilingual Instruction.* Final report to the Office of Education, Division of Bilingual Education. Pullman, WA: State Evaluation Office.

MCDERMOTT, R. and ROTH, D. R. (1979) 'The social organization of behavior: Interactional approaches.' *Annual Review of Anthropology*, 7, 321–45.

MCDERMOTT, R. P., GOLDMAN, S. V. and VARENNE, H. (1984) 'When school goes home: Some problems in the organization of homework.' *Teacher's College Record*, 85, 381–409.

MCGUIRE, D. E. and LYONS, J. S. (1985) 'A transcontextual model for intervention with problems of school underachievement.' *The American Journal of Family Therapy*, 13, 37–45.

MELARAGNO, R. J., KEESLING, W. J., LYONS, M. F., ROBBINS, A. E. and SMITH, A. G. (1981) *Parents and Federal Education Programs Volume I: The Nature, Causes and Consequences of Parental Involvement.* Research report submitted to the United States Department of Education. Washington, DC: TM-6974-004/00.

MICHAELS, S. (1981) 'Children's narrative styles and differential access to literacy.' *Language in Society*, 10, 423–43.

MOLL, L. C. and DIAZ, S. (1987) 'Change as a goal of educational research.' *Anthropology and Education Quarterly*, 18, 300–11.

OGBU, J. (1978), *Minority Education and Caste.* New York: Academic Press.

OGBU, J. (1981a) 'Societal forces as a context of ghetto children's school failure.' In L. FEAGAN and D. CLARK (Eds) *The Language of Children Reared in poverty: Implications for Evaluation and Intervention* (pp. 256–71). New York: Academic Press.

OGBU, J. (1981b) 'Origins of human competence: A cultural-ecological perspective.' *Child Development*, 52, 413–29.

PESHKIN, A. (1982) 'The researcher and subjectivity: Reflections on an ethnography of school and community.' In G. SPINDLER (Ed.), *Doing the Ethnography of Schooling* (pp. 20–46). New York: Holt, Rinehart and Winston.

PESHKIN, A. (1988) 'In search of subjectivity — one's own.' *Educational Researcher*, 17, 17–22.

PORTES, A. and TRUELOVE, C. (1987) 'Making sense of diversity: Recent research on Hispanic minorities in the US.' *Annual Review of Sociology*, 13, 359–85.

REVICKI, D. A. (1981) *The Relationship among Socioeconomic Status, Home Environment, Parent Involvement, Child Self-concept and Child Achievement.* (ERIC – 206–645).

RUEDA, R and MEHAN, H. (1986) 'Metacognition and passing: Strategic interactions in the lives of students with learning disabilities.' *Anthropology and Education Quarterly*, 17, 145–65.

RUMBERGER, R. W. (1983) 'High school dropouts.' *Review of Educational Research*, 57, 101–27.

RUMBERGER, R. W. (1987) 'Dropping out of high school: The influence of race, sex, and family background.' *American Educational Research Journal*, 20, 199–220.

SCHIEFFELIN, B. and COCHRAN-SMITH, M. (1984) 'Learning to read culturally: Literacy before schooling.' In H. GOELMAN, A. OBERG and F. SMITH (Eds), *Awakening to Literacy* (pp. 3–23), London: Heinemann Educational Books.

SCHIEFFELIN, B. B. and GILMORE, P. (Eds) (1986) *The Acquisition of Literacy: Ethnographic Perspectives.* Norwood NJ: Ablex.

SCRIBNER, S. and COLE M. (1981) *The Psychology of Literacy.* Cambridge, MA: Harvard University Press.

SKEELS, H and DYE, H. (1959) 'A study of the effects of differential stimulation on mentally retarded children.' *Proceedings of the American Association on Mental Deficiency,* (pp. 114–36).

SMITH, D. (1986) 'The anthropology of literacy acquisition.' In B. SCHIEFFELIN and P. GILMORE (Eds), *The Acquisition of Literacy: Ethnographic Perspectives* (pp. 261–76). Norwood, NJ: Ablex.

SPINDLER, G. (Ed.) (1955) *Anthropology and Education,* Stanford, CA: Stanford University Press.

SPINDLER, G. (Ed.) (1982) *Doing the Ethnography of Schooling.* Stanford, CA: Holt, Rinehart and Winston.

SPRADLEY J. P. (1979) *The Ethnographic Interview.* New York: Holt, Rinehart and Winston.

STOCKTON, G. (1960) *La Carpinteria.* Carpinteria, CA: The Carpinteria Valley Historical Society.

SUPER, C. M. and HARKNESS, S. (Eds) (1980) *Anthropological Perspectives on Child Development: New Directions for Child Development.* San Francisco, CA: Jossey-Bass.

TANNEN, D. (Ed.) (1982) *Spoken and Written Language.* Norwood, NJ: Ablex.

THARP, R. and GALLIMORE, R. (1988) *Arousing Mind to Life: Teaching, Learning and Schooling in Social Context.* Cambridge, MA: Cambridge University Press.

THARP, R., JORDAN, C. and O'DONNEL, C. (1980) 'Behavioral community psychology: A cross disciplinary example with theoretical implications.' Paper presented at the annual meeting of the American Psychological Association, Montreal.

TIZARD, J., SCHOFIELD, W. N. and HEWISON, J. (1982) 'Collaboration between teachers and parents in assisting children's reading.' *British Journal of Educational Psychology,* 52, 1–11.

TRUEBA, H. T. (1984) 'The forms, functions and values of literacy: Reading for survival.' *NABE Journal,* 9, 21–39.

TRUEBA, H. T. (Ed.) (1987) *Success and Failure: Learning and the Linguistic Minority Student.* Cambridge, MA: Newbury House.

TRUEBA, H. T. (1989) *Raising Silent Voices: Educating the Linguistic Minority for the 21st Century.* New York: Newbury House.

UNITED STATES CENSUS BUREAU (1981) 1980 Census data for Carpinteria, California.

VANDERSLICE, V. (1984) 'Empowerment: A definition in process.' *Human Ecology Forum,* 14, 1–4.

VARENNE, H. and McDERMOTT, R. (1986) 'Why Sheila can read: Structure and indeterminancy in the reproduction of familial literacy.' In B. SCHIEFFELIN and P. GILMORE (Eds), *The Acquisition of Literacy: Ethnographnic Perspectives* (pp. 261–75). Norwood, NJ: Ablex.

VYGOTSKY, L. S. (1978) *Mind in Society: The Development of Higher Psychological Processes.* Ed. and trans by M. COLE, V. JOHN-STEINER, S. SCRIBNER and E. SOUBERMAN. Cambridge, MA: Harvard University Press.

WALKER, C. L. (1987) 'Hispanic achievement: Old views and new perspectives.' In H. T. TRUEBA (Ed.), *Success or Failure? Learning and the Language Minority Students* (pp. 15–32). Cambridge, MA: Newbury House.

WALLER, W. (1932) *The Sociology of Teaching.* New York: Wiley.

WARREN, R. L. (1988) 'Cooperation and conflict between parents and teachers: A comparative study of three elementary schools.' In H. TRUEBA and C. DELGADO-GAITAN (Eds), *School and Society: Learning Content through Culture* (pp. 137–62). New York: Praeger.

WEISNER, T. S. (1976) 'Urban-rural differences in African children's performance on cognitive and memory tasks.' *Ethos,* 4, 223–50.

WEISNER, T. S. (1979) 'Urban-rural differences in sociable and disruptive behavior of Kenya children.' *Ethnology,* 18, 153–72.

WEISNER, T. S. (1984) 'Ecocultural niches of middle childhood: A cross-cultural perspective.' In W. A. COLLINS (Ed.), *Development during Middle Childhood: The Years from Six to Twelve* (pp. 335–69). Washington, DC: National Academy of Sciences Press.

WEISNER, T. S., GALLIMORE, R. and JORDAN, C. (1988) 'Unpackaging cultural effects on classroom learning: Hawaiian peer assistance and child-generated activity.' *Anthropology and Education Quarterly,* 9, 327–53.

WERTSCH, J. (1981) *Concept of Activity in Soviet Psychology.* New York: M. E. Sharpe.

WERTSCH, J. (1985) *Vygotsky and the Social Formation of the Mind.* Cambridge, MA: Harvard University Press.

WOLCOTT, H. F. (1987) 'On ethnography intent.' In G. SPINDLER and L. SPINDLER (Eds), *Interpretive Ethnography of Education at Home and Abroad* (pp. 38–60). Hillsdale, NJ: Lawrence Erlbaum Associates.

WOLCOTT, H. F. (1988) ' "Problem finding" in qualitative research.' In H. T. TRUEBA and C. DELGADO-GAITAN (Eds), *School in Society: Learning Content through Culture* (pp. 11–35). New York: Praeger.

Index